W9-AOY-132

The New Bread

GREAT GLUTEN-FREE BAKING

Copyright © 2015 by Schiffer Publishing, Ltd.

Library of Congress Control Number: 2015952661

Originally published as Nytt Bröd: Baka Gott Utan Gluten
by Forma Books, Malmo, Sweden ©2013 Maria Blohm, Jessica
Frej, and Ica Bokforlag.

Translated from the Swedish by Carol Huebscher Rhoades

All rights reserved. No part of this work may be
reproduced or used in any form   or by any means—
graphic, electronic, or mechanical, including
photocopying or information storage and retrieval
systems—without written permission from the publisher.

The scanning, uploading, and distribution of this book
or any part thereof via the Internet or via any other
means without the permission of the publisher is illegal
and punishable by law. Please purchase only authorized
editions and do not participate in or encourage
the electronic piracy of copyrighted materials.
"Schiffer," "Schiffer Publishing, Ltd. & Design,"
and the "Design of pen and inkwell" are registered
trademarks of Schiffer Publishing, Ltd.

Cover design by Molly Shields
Type set in Montada & Courier

ISBN: 978-0-7643-4968-3
Printed in China

Published by Schiffer Publishing, Ltd.
4880 Lower Valley Road
Atglen, PA 19310
Phone: (610) 593-1777; Fax: (610) 593-2002
E-mail: Info@schifferbooks.com

For our complete selection of fine books on this
and related subjects, please visit our website at
www.schifferbooks.com. You may also write for a
free catalog.

This book may be purchased from the publisher.
Please try your bookstore first.

We are always looking for people to write books on new
and related subjects. If you have an idea for a book,
please contact us at proposals@schifferbooks.com.

Schiffer Publishing's titles are available at special
discounts for bulk purchases for sales promotions or
premiums. Special editions, including personalized
covers, corporate imprints, and excerpts can be created
in large quantities for special needs. For more
information, contact the publisher.

JESSICA FREJ & MARIA BLOHM
PHOTOS FILIPPA TREDAL

The New Bread

GREAT GLUTEN-FREE BAKING

Table of contents

Preface

We think that this is the world's most important book because it is a book about sandwiches - good sandwiches.

It was precisely the idea of good sandwiches that led us to our vision: everyone should be able to eat good bread. Shouldn't that be obvious? However, it isn't always the case for everyone these days. A large group of people don't get to eat good sandwiches.

This book offers anyone who is gluten-intolerant good bread that is moist and long-lasting, and, for those of you who can tolerate gluten, variety and more options in your bread repertoire.

The need for this book became evident on the day when we first met at a café to bounce around ideas. Maria (who is fine with gluten) could easily eat any of the café's excellent offerings while Jessica (who is gluten-intolerant) had to satisfy herself with a mediocre cup of coffee. The sad thing is that Jessica didn't even note that there wasn't something for her because she was so used to this situation. Instead, it was Maria who noticed it, and it became very obvious that good bread is necessary for everyone who eats.

We began thinking about why no one had previously baked good, moist gluten-free bread with pure raw ingredients and without additives. Why is everything based on wheat flour mixtures? Is it because it isn't possible or just because no one has taken the time to try?

Maria, who has experience in the baking world and who, for several years, was an instructor for bread baking, had gotten questions about this throughout her baking career. The prevailing notion seems to be that it really isn't possible to bake gluten-free bread that would in any way resemble regular bread. We decided that we had to give it a try and take the time necessary to do it. We wouldn't compromise - the bread would have to be so good that everyone would want to eat it.

Our vision is even bigger than that. With this book, we want to change your concept of bread. Does bread have to contain gluten to be good when there are actually several kinds of gluten-free flours and raw ingredients other than the three - wheat, rye, and barley - that contain gluten? Wouldn't it be nice to create breads only with pure raw ingredients offering new options for your taste buds and even your nutritional intake? (See page 141 for nutritional information.)

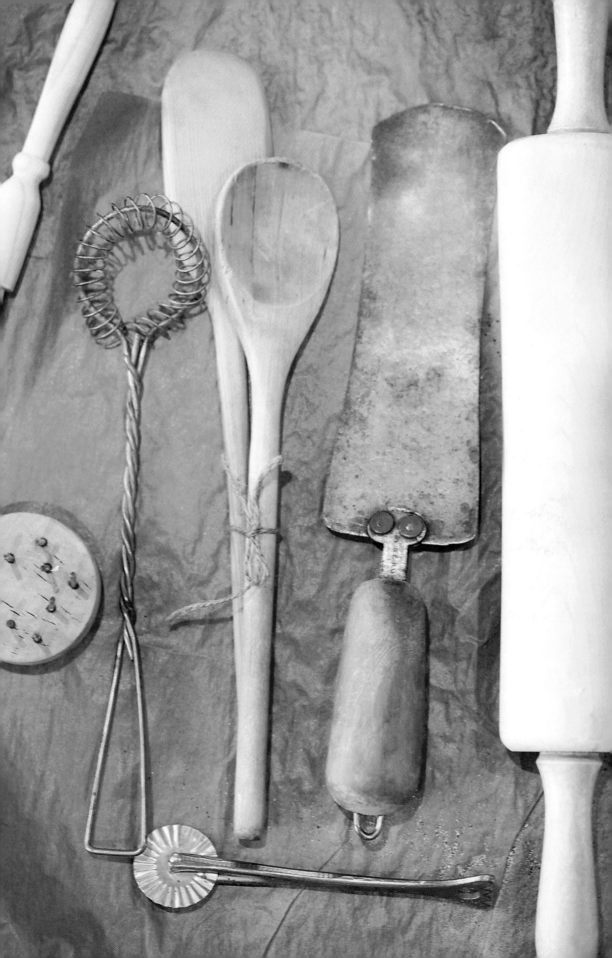

In our culture, we've grown up with bread and sandwiches. Being able to have a sandwich is something fundamental in our lives. If we are just a little hungry, we eat a sandwich. If you want a little something, you eat a sandwich. You can eat a sandwich for lunch and a sandwich after exercise, a sandwich in the morning and one for an evening snack. It is always time for a sandwich. Imagine then, that, from one day to the next, suddenly you can't have a sandwich. Or, you can find a sandwich, but it doesn't look or taste like one.

That is precisely what happened to Jessica. When she was twelve years old, she was diagnosed with celiac disease. It was a huge event that changed her everyday life, and the worst was that she could no longer eat sandwiches. It was eleven years before Jessica was once again able to eat good bread that tasted and felt like real bread – it was when we began to work on this book and lucked out, baking bread that was really good.

It has been an unbelievably exciting journey to create this book. We came from two different backgrounds and have taught each other much along the way. We hope that our readers will try our recipes and enjoy the bread and everything else as much as we have. This is bread for everyone!

With wishes for a lot of pleasure and enjoyment!

Jessica and Maria

What Happens to the Dough?

Gluten-free bread is not something one usually associates with the words *airy* and *chewy*. The expression "the bread you could kill someone with" is one that frequently comes out when people talk about the gluten-free bread they've eaten.

It would be easier to understand why gluten-free bread is most often not at all like bread baked, for example, with wheat flour, if you understand a little about the process that occurs when bread is baked. There are two proteins in wheat flour – gluten and gliadin – which influence the baking characteristics. When flour is mixed with water and kneaded, the two proteins join and build gluten strands. With a long rising time or through kneading these strands become strong and elastic and build a network within the dough. This network holds up the bread like a skeleton, which means that it can rise properly without collapsing. This is how we obtain chewy, airy bread that is pleasant to eat.

Because those who are gluten-intolerant cannot metabolize the little strands of gliadin (an element of the gluten threads), it is also impossible to build the same structure in gluten-free bread. We have to think in a completely different way when we want to bake without gluten.

The most common types of grain contain a lot of starches, approximately 70-80 percent, and even the starches build up the bread's stability and crumb. The starches form small skeins of threads and can also bind large amounts of liquid, which we add for moister bread. These starches are also found in a number of foods that are gluten-free, for example, potatoes, rice, and corn. Dough that contains wheat must be kneaded for a period of time to develop the tough, durable gluten strands that prevent flat and heavy bread. Bread without gluten doesn't gain anything from a long time in the dough blender or mixer but can be whisked together by hand or processed for just a few minutes in the machine.

In order for the gluten-free bread to be ready without being gluey or heavy inside, the starches have to coagulate. When bread is baked, the starches and liquid are heated and a chemical reaction called gelatinization occurs. The temperature rises and the starches absorb the liquid. When that has gone on for a while, the starches dissolve and the liquid fills with starch molecules. This allows the mixture of liquid and starch to thicken, which, quite simply said, transforms the dough into bread that has a set shape and can be cut.

To bake gluten-free bread, if one hasn't done it earlier, means that, to some extent, you have to free yourself from your previous knowledge and your concepts and ideas about how to bake bread. It doesn't work at all to simply substitute gluten-free flour for wheat flour because they, for obvious reasons, won't behave the same way.

We have built up our breads with the help of starches, but also with gel that composes, for example, psyllium seeds. Binding the liquid is also important so that the bread doesn't dry out, and we accomplished that with the help of various liquid-binding raw ingredients.

Ingredients

Editor's note:
The ingredients in the following recipes are listed by weight, not volume, because baking gluten-free requires precise measurements. A digital kitchen scale is recommended.

Many of the ingredients in these recipes can be purchased in organic and whole food grocery stores, or can be ordered online. Molasses can be substituted for Swedish light or dark syrup.

You will recognize many of the ingredients listed in this book. Here are a few of them that you can easily mix. Several products, such as cornmeal and cornstarch/Maizena, are produced from the same raw materials but yield very different results.

Buckwheat
It is easy to believe from the name that buckwheat is related to common wheat, but that is not the case. Buckwheat is a plant that is closely related to, for example, rhubarb. This means that it is naturally free of gluten. Buckwheat is rich in B-vitamins, contains potassium, magnesium, phosphorus, iron, and is very filling.

Buckwheat flakes are whole buckwheat that has been steamed and rolled into flakes. They add structure and a full grain feel to bread and also help bind the liquid to make the bread more moist.

Buckwheat flour is produced from buckwheat husks ground to flour. For obvious reasons, buckwheat flour does not react the same way as wheat flour, but still has very good baking qualities and, for that reason, we use it in many of our recipes.

Corn
Corn is a species of grass that can grow up to 20 feet high. The corn we commonly eat is called sweet corn. Corn contains essential fats, protein, magnesium, iron, potassium, zinc, B-3,and a number of antioxidants.

Cornmeal is ground from whole corn and lends a good flavor and color to bread. Cornmeal has somewhat more binding power than polenta.

Cornstarch/Maizena is produced from the inner part of the kernel. The starch functions as a stabilizer and cannot be broken out of cornmeal.

Polenta is small grain that does not bind as well as cornstarch but it does create structure and gives bread a good taste and color.

Potatoes

Potato flour is, in large part, pure starch. It functions as a stabilizer.

Psyllium

When it comes to gluten-free baking, almost nothing is better at binding with the liquid than psyllium. It makes bread moist and its gelatinous character stabilizes the bread. Instead of using, for example, xanthan gum and guar flour, which are added to a number of gluten-free recipes, and are expensive and difficult to obtain, we use psyllium seeds in various forms.

Psyllium seeds are also called horse flower seeds and come from plants of the plantago family. The whole black psyllium seed is high in fiber, which absorbs the liquid and creates a mucilaginous gel that enables the intestines to function better.

Psyllium seed husks are a part of our substitutions for gluten because they bind with the liquid and stabilize the dough. Psyllium seed husks are high in fiber.

Fiber husks consist of pulverized psyllium seed husks and have almost the same effect as the coarser psyllium seed husks. They give the dough a smoother look and feel.

Rosehip powder

Rosehip powder is produced from deseeded and dried rosehips that are then ground to powder. Rosehips are rich in vitamin C and antioxidants and add a good, sour flavor to bread.

Buckwheat flour

Fiber husks

Buckwheat flakes

Psyllium seeds

Psyllium seed husks

Editor's note:
Bread spices - a variety of spices can be used depending on your taste: anise, fennel, cumin, coriander, Seville orange peel, cardamom, cinnamon, ginger, cloves, saffron, and vanilla

Fibrex - a gluten-free fiber derived from processed sugar beets. Also called NutraFiber.

Syrup - Swedish syrup is either light or dark sweet beet syrup (molasses can be substituted for syrup); available from Scandinavian grocers. Imported by the Chicago Importing Co., Elgin, IL 60123.

Vanilla sugar: a powdered mixture of confectioner's sugar and vanilla essence.

Yeast - the yeast recommended in this book is compressed fresh yeast, available at most grocers in the refrigerated section.

Cornmeal

Cornstarch

Potato flour

Polenta

Rosehip powder

About the Recipes

We want you to have good results with the breads you bake and to do so every time! We made a lot of mistakes, but that has given us the experience we want to share with you. Follow our recipes exactly for the best results.

In order for you to do well with your gluten-free baking, the measurements in the recipes are by weight and not amount. Flour has a tendency to compact differently every time you measure it, so, to be sure that the bread is exactly the same every time, we weigh the flour. You should do that also. A digital kitchen scale is a good investment and will help you be successful.

The very smallest measurements, such as a few grams of salt, bread spices or the like, are given by amount because not all kitchen scales measure a few grams very accurately. Don't forget to clear the weight between measuring each of the ingredients and to pour the ingredients straight out of the package. That makes the process faster and saves you extra dish washing. Baking gluten-free is not the same as baking with wheat flour, and there are a few ground rules that you need to become familiar with.

- You can mix gluten-free dough by hand with the help of a whisk or in a mixer but use the dough hook on the machine.

- If the dough has buckwheat flour, mix the dough for about 5 minutes with an electric mixer or with the dough hook on a stand mixer (Kitchen Aide).

- Fiber husks and psyllium seed husks have a tendency to clump together when they come in contact with liquid. It is important to incorporate those ingredients into the dough quickly, as soon as they are added.

- If the dough seems loose, don't do your own experimenting. Just wait 10 minutes. The dough will cohere better after resting a while.

- All the recipes use cool liquid for the dough and a rather small amount of yeast. The bread will be much better if you allow a long rising time. Let the bread take its time – it is well worth the time when it comes to taste.

- Some of our breads can be frozen but most do not keep especially well in the freezer. Our recipes are for rather small amounts. It is better to bake an amount that you can eat in a short time rather than extra that has to be stored in the freezer.

- Most breads are best a few hours, or even the next day, after coming out of the oven. You need to let the bread cool and stabilize before you cut it; otherwise, the bread will seem doughy and feel a little gelatinous. There are exceptions, of course, such as croissants and butter rolls that are best fresh from the oven. This information has been noted in the individual recipes.

- Some of the recipes contain milk products. We have tried substituting lactose-free buttermilk, soy yogurt, or similar milk-free products for buttermilk. The results were just the same. If you are lactose-intolerant or allergic to milk products just substitute the product you usually use for those in the recipe.

RECIPES

The Chimney Sweep

The chimney sweep loaf, with plenty of flavor and sweetness, was inspired by black rye bread. The bread is quick and easy to bake and keeps moist and fresh for several days.

- Heat oven to 350°F.
- Butter a bread pan that holds about 1½ quarts.
- Mix all the ingredients together well and pour the batter into the pan. Sprinkle with buckwheat flour.
- Bake for 45 minutes on the lower shelf of the oven.
- Let bread cool completely before you cut it.

<u>MAKES 1 LOAF</u>

21.16 OUNCES (600 G)
  BUTTERMILK

7.05 OUNCES (200 G)
  DARK SYRUP

1 TEASPOON BAKING SODA

1.06 OUNCES (30 G)
  ROSEHIP POWDER

9.17 OUNCES (260 G)
  BUCKWHEAT FLOUR

1.41 OUNCES (40 G)
  SOY FLOUR

0.71 OUNCES (20 G)
  PSYLLIUM SEED HUSKS

2 TEASPOONS SALT

2 TABLESPOONS BREAD
  SPICES

BUTTER FOR THE PAN

BUCKWHEAT FLOUR TO
  SPRINKLE OVER THE
  BREAD

Fiber Rolls

Unsweetened rolls, filled with nutritious fibers that are good for your stomach and keep you satisfied longer. These are perfect before or after an exercise session or for a healthy breakfast. The rolls will stay fresh for several days.

- Use a whisk to blend the milk, yeast, and canola oil until the yeast dissolves.
- Add remaining ingredients. Using a stand mixer with a dough hook, knead the dough for 5 minutes.
- Cover bowl with plastic wrap and let the dough rise for about 2 hours.
- Heat oven to 450-475°F.
- Use two spoons to scoop out 8 rolls of dough onto a baking sheet covered with baking parchment.
- Bake the rolls for 25 minutes.
- Cool rolls completely before cutting.

MAKES 8 ROLLS

19.40 OUNCES (550 G)
  COLD MILK

0.71 OUNCES (20 G)
  YEAST

0.88 OUNCES (25 G)
  CANOLA OIL

0.35 OUNCES (10 G)
  WHOLE BLACK PSYLLIUM
  SEEDS

0.88 OUNCES (25 G)
  FIBREX

3.53 OUNCES (100 G)
  HULLED OATS

2.47 OUNCES (70 G)
  BUCKWHEAT FLOUR

1.41 OUNCES (40 G)
  SOY FLOUR

¼ TEASPOON BREAD SPICES

½ TEASPOON SALT

0.71 OUNCES (20 G)
  PSYLLIUM SEED HUSKS

Butternut Squash Marmalade
with Lemon and Ginger

*Here's a pretty autumn marmalade that will
make you happy with its glad orange color and
stimulating flavor of ginger. Pour it into
small, pretty jars and give to friends and
family around Halloween. It will also be a
success on the cheese board.*

- Cut the squash into cubes about ¾ x ¾
  inches.
- Put the squash and sugar into a saucepan.
  Bring to boil and then simmer on low heat
  for 40 minutes.
- Mash the soft squash with a potato masher or
  in the mixer.
- Finely grate the lemon peel and mix the
  lemon peel and juice into the marmalade.
- Finely chop the peeled ginger and add to the
  marmalade while it is still warm.

MAKES 1 BATCH
17.64 OUNCES (500 G)
  BUTTERNUT SQUASH CUT
  INTO SMALL PIECES
14.11 OUNCES (400 G)
  SUGAR
1 LEMON, PEEL AND JUICE
1¼-INCH-LONG PIECE OF
  FRESH, PEELED GINGER

TIPS!
It is important to sterilize
the jars thoroughly. Wash and
rinse the jars well or fill
them with boiling water to
kill bacteria. Fill the jars
to the brim and make sure the
marmalade is piping hot when
it is poured. Seal the lid
immediately to create a vacuum
so the marmalade will keep
longer.

Syrup Limpa

Syrup limpa is a little underrated but oh so beloved. For Swedes, it is a reminder of childhood with cheese and warm chocolate at the kitchen table or on an outing in the woods.

- Mix the milk, yeast, syrup, buckwheat flour, cornstarch, salt, and bread spices to a smooth dough.
- Quickly blend in the psyllium seed husks.
- Cover the bowl with plastic wrap and let dough rise for about 2 hours.
- Turn dough out onto floured work surface. Shape the dough into a round loaf and sprinkle with buckwheat flour.
- Place the loaf on a baking sheet covered with baking parchment.
- Let loaf rise for 30 minutes.
- Heat oven to 400°F.
- Bake in center of oven for 45 minutes.
- Cool bread completely before cutting.

MAKES 1 LOAF

17.64 OUNCES (500 G) COLD MILK

0.17 OUNCES (20 G) YEAST

3.53 OUNCES (100 G) DARK SYRUP (OR MOLASSES)

10.58 OUNCES (300 G) BUCKWHEAT FLOUR

1.76 OUNCES (50 G) CORNSTARCH

2 TEASPOONS SALT

1 TEASPOON BREAD SPICES

1.41 OUNCES (40 G) PSYLLIUM SEED HUSKS

BUCKWHEAT FLOUR FOR WORK SURFACE

BUCKWHEAT FLOUR FOR SPRINKLING OVER THE LOAF

TIP!
Make your own hot chocolate!

10.14 ounces (3 DL) milk
3.38 ounces (1 DL) cream
1.76 ounces (50 g) dark chocolate, 70%
1 teaspoon vanilla sugar

Heat milk and cream. Add the chocolate and let melt. Add vanilla sugar to taste.

Raisin Buns

Lovely buns with firm, dark crust and moist crumb with sweet raisins. Good with butter and cheese for a walk in the woods or served at the breakfast table.

- Whisk together the yeast, milk, and syrup.
- Add the bread spices, buckwheat flour, salt, and psyllium seed husks and blend to a smooth dough.
- Mix in the raisins.
- Cover the bowl with plastic and let dough rise for about 2 hours.
- Oil your hands and shape dough into 10 buns.
- Place rolls on a baking sheet covered with baking parchment and sprinkle each bun with buckwheat flour.
- Let buns rise on the pan for about 1 hour.
- Heat oven to 435°F.
- Bake in center of oven for 30 min.
- Cool buns completely before cutting.

MAKES 10 BUNS

0.17 OUNCES (20 G) YEAST
17.64 OUNCES (500 G) MILK
1.76 OUNCES (50 G) DARK SYRUP
1 TEASPOON BREAD SPICES
8.47 OUNCES (240 G) BUCKWHEAT FLOUR
1½ TEASPOONS SALT
1.06 OUNCES (30 G) PSYLLIUM SEED HUSKS
2.12 OUNCES (60 G) RAISINS
CANOLA OIL FOR HANDS WHILE SHAPING BUNS
BUCKWHEAT FLOUR TO SPRINKLE OVER THE BUNS

Seeded Crisp Bread

A really light, crispy, and full-flavored, delicate bread, loaded with good, nutritious seeds. If you store the crisp bread in a dry and airy container, it will keep for several weeks.

- Blend all the ingredients in the mixer until dough is smooth.
- Cover the bowl with plastic and let rest for 2 hours.
- Divide the dough into two.
- Roll out the dough on baking parchment until as thin as possible.
- Bake in the oven at 350°F for 30-40 minutes or until crisp.
- Turn off oven and let the bread dry in the oven with the door ajar.

MAKES 2 LARGE FLAT-BREADS

7.05 OUNCES (200 G) WATER

1.23 OUNCES (35 G) SUNFLOWER SEEDS

1.06 OUNCES (30 G) PUMPKIN SEEDS

0.35 OUNCES (10 G) CHIA SEEDS

0.35 OUNCES (10 G) BLACK PSYLLIUM SEEDS

1.41 OUNCES (40 G) ALMOND FLOUR

0.25 OUNCES (7 G) YEAST

½ TEASPOON SALT

0.42 OUNCES (12 G) FIBER HUSKS

Coarse Bread

This bread is moist, keeps well, is rich flavored and has a nice chew. Good together with, for example, homemade liver paste and pickles.

- Blend all the ingredients together until the dough is smooth and rather loose.
- Pour the dough into the buttered bread pan (about 1½ quart).
- Sprinkle the top with buckwheat flakes.
- Let dough rise for about 2 hours.
- Heat oven to 350°F and bake bread for about 75 minutes.
- Cool bread completely before cutting it – waiting until the next day is recommended.

MAKES 1 LOAF

21.16 OUNCES (600 G) COLD WATER

0.35 OUNCES (10 G) YEAST

3.53 OUNCES (100 G) SUNFLOWER SEEDS

1.06 OUNCES (30 G) FLAX SEEDS

1.23 OUNCES (35 G) MELON SEEDS

1.76 OUNCES (50 G) DARK SYRUP

0.17 OUNCES (20 G) ROSEHIP POWDER

1 TEASPOON BREAD SPICES

1 TEASPOON SALT

1.76 OUNCES (50 G) BUCKWHEAT FLAKES

2.12 OUNCES (60 G) SOY FLOUR

5.64 OUNCES (160 G) BUCKWHEAT FLOUR

0.88 OUNCES (25 G) PSYLLIUM SEED HUSKS

BUTTER FOR THE PAN

BUCKWHEAT FLAKES TO SPRINKLE OVER THE LOAF

Liver Paste

Making your own liver paste is really easy and it's fun to share. Best of all, you know exactly what's in the paste so you can be sure there is no gluten or other unwanted food additives.

- Heat oven to 300°F.
- Peel and slice the onion.
- Place all the ingredients in a food processor and mix on high for a couple of minutes.
- Pour the batter into a buttered 1½-quart pan. Set the pan in a larger ovenproof pan and pour warm water into the larger pan to form a water bath.
- Bake on lower shelf of oven for about 50 minutes.
- Remove the small pan from the water bath and let the liver paste cool.
- Turn the liver paste out of the pan onto a platter or serve directly from the baking pan.

MAKES ABOUT 16 SLICES

1.76 OUNCES (50 G) YELLOW ONION (1 SMALL ONION)

7.05 OUNCES (200 G) CHICKEN LIVER

7.05 OUNCES (200 G) GROUND BEEF

1 EGG

3.38 OUNCES (1 DL) WHIPPING CREAM

2 TABLESPOONS POTATO FLOUR

½ TABLESPOON SALT

1 TABLESPOON BROWN SUGAR

1 TEASPOON BLACK PEPPER

¼ TEASPOON NUTMEG

1 TABLESPOON RUM

Potato and Goji Berry Bread

A moist bread that is pretty, with red flecks of goji berries. Goji berries contain loads of antioxidants, particularly zeaxanthin, which is good for your eyes.

<u>MAKES 1 LOAF</u>
17.64 OUNCES (500 G) BUTTERMILK
0.71 OUNCES (20 G) YEAST
1.76 OUNCES (50 G) LIGHT SYRUP
1.23 OUNCES (35 G) CORNSTARCH
1½ TEASPOONS SALT
3.53 OUNCES (100 G) POTATOES, PEELED, AND
  COARSELY CHOPPED (ABOUT 2 POTATOES)
0.88 OUNCES (25 G) GOJI BERRIES
1.76 OUNCES (50 G) CORNMEAL
0.88 OUNCES (25 G) BUCKWHEAT FLOUR
0.71 OUNCES (20 G) PSYLLIUM SEED HUSKS
BUCKWHEAT FLOUR FOR WORK SURFACE
BUCKWHEAT FLOUR FOR SPRINKLING OVER LOAF

- Mix all the ingredients until dough is blended evenly.
- Cover bowl with plastic wrap and let dough rise for 2 hours.
- Turn dough onto a floured work surface and shape into a round loaf.
- Sprinkle buckwheat flour over the loaf.
- Let rise for about 30 minutes.
- Place on a baking sheet covered with baking parchment.
- Heat oven to 350°F. Bake bread for 45 minutes.
- Cool bread completely before cutting.

Carrot Bread in a Pan

This bread is perfect for breakfast or to serve with soup. Cut it into squares and eat with your favorite spread.

- Whisk the water, yeast and honey together until yeast and honey are dissolved.
- Stirring continually, add the cornmeal, rice flour, buckwheat flour, salt, and psyllium seed husks.
- Shred the carrot and mix into the dough.
- Pour the dough into a shallow ovenproof pan lined with baking parchment.
- Sprinkle the sunflower seeds over the loaf.
- Let rise for 1½ hours.
- Heat oven to 435°F and bake bread for about 30 minutes.

MAKES 1 LOAF

17.64 OUNCES (500 G) WATER

0.71 OUNCES (20 G) YEAST

0.35 OUNCES (10 G) HONEY

1.76 OUNCES (50 G) CORNMEAL

3.53 OUNCES (100 G) RICE FLOUR

7.05 OUNCES (200 G) BUCKWHEAT FLOUR

1 TEASPOON SALT

0.71 OUNCES (20 G) PSYLLIUM SEED HUSKS

2.47 OUNCES (70 G) CARROTS (ABOUT 1 CARROT)

1.76 OUNCES (50 G) SUNFLOWER SEEDS TO SPRINKLE OVER THE BREAD.

wild Yeast

Producing your own yeast is rather easy but it does take a little time. When you use wild yeast, the bread takes on a different character than with commercial yeast. For a recipe using wild yeast, see our sourdough bread on page 42.

- Mix the ingredients in a clean glass jar with a loose-fitting lid. It is important that the jar not seal completely because otherwise the jar could explode when the wild yeast begins fermenting.
- Place the jar somewhere slightly warmer than room temperature, next to the stove for example, on a radiator, or above the refrigerator.
- Shake the jar morning and evening for 4 – 6 days. The wild yeast is ready when the figs or apricots have floated to the surface and are covered with a white scum. When the carbonic acid rises to the surface, it will bubble like a carbonated drink. The wild yeast should have a flavor similar to wine, beer, or alcohol.
- Sieve out the fruit and save the liquid. If you don't want to use all the liquid immediately, save it in a clean glass jar in the refrigerator. The yeast should last about 2 months.
- When ready to use wild yeast that has been stored in the refrigerator, take it out the evening beforehand so it can revive at room temperature.

MAKES 1 PORTION

4.41 OUNCES (125 G) DRIED APRICOTS OR FIGS

1.76 OUNCES (50 G) HONEY

0.88 OUNCES (25 G) SUGAR

8.82 OUNCES (250 G) LUKEWARM WATER

Sourdough Bread

This bread takes its time but the time is repaid with extra flavor. The bread, with its characteristic crust and soft crumb, has a completely unique flavor thanks to the wild yeast and is well worth every moment spent on it.

Step 1

- Mix the wild yeast, rice and buckwheat flours in a bowl.
- Blend the dough for 5 minutes in a stand mixer.
- Cover the bowl with plastic wrap and let rise for about 4 hours.

Step 2

- Mix the dough from step 1 with the remaining ingredients.
- Blend the dough for 5 minutes in a stand mixer with the dough hook.
- Cover the bowl with plastic wrap and let rise for about 4 hours.

Step 3

- Mix the dough from step 2 with the remaining ingredients.
- Blend the dough for 5 minutes in a stand mixer with the dough hook.
- Cover the bowl with plastic wrap and let rise for about 10 hours.
- Heat oven to 525°F.
- Shape the dough into a round loaf and sprinkle with buckwheat flour and place on baking sheet covered with baking parchment.
- Bake for 30 – 40 minutes, lowering oven heat to 435°F after 15 – 20 minutes.
- Cool bread completely before cutting it.

MAKES 1 LOAF

4.41 OUNCES (125 G) WILD YEAST LIQUID (SEE PAGE 41)

2.82 OUNCES (80 G) RICE FLOUR

2.82 OUNCES (80 G) BUCKWHEAT FLOUR

ALL THE DOUGH FROM STEP 1

3.53 OUNCES (100 G) COLD WATER

1.76 OUNCES (50 G) BUCKWHEAT FLOUR

1.76 OUNCES (50 G) CORNMEAL

½ TABLESPOON PSYLLIUM SEED HUSKS

ALL THE DOUGH FROM STEPS 1 AND 2

17.64 OUNCES (500 G) COLD WATER

7.05 OUNCES (200 G) BUCKWHEAT FLOUR

5.29 OUNCES (150 G) CORNMEAL

2 TABLESPOONS PSYLLIUM SEED HUSKS

1 TEASPOON SALT

BUCKWHEAT FLOUR TO SPRINKLE OVER THE BREAD

TIP!
If the dough doesn't rise well, put it in a somewhat warmer place, for example, in the oven with the door closed or above the refrigerator.

Flaxseed Rolls

Flaxseeds contain both nutritious fiber and omega-3, and, when combined with rolled oats, yield a good flavor to these moist and long-lasting buns.

- Whisk the yeast and water together.
- Blend in the rolled oats, flaxseeds, buckwheat flour, salt, and psyllium seed husks.
- Cover the bowl with plastic wrap and let rise for about 2 hours.
- Heat oven to 475°F.
- Shape the rolls using two spoons and divide them onto two baking sheets covered with baking parchment. Sprinkle some flaxseeds over each roll.
- Let rise for about 30 minutes.
- Bake for 25 minutes.
- Cool rolls completely before cutting.

<u>MAKES 10 ROLLS</u>

0.71 OUNCES (20 G) YEAST

28.22 OUNCES (800 G) COLD WATER

1.76 OUNCES (50 G) ROLLED OATS

0.53 OUNCES (15 G) FLAXSEEDS

11.64 OUNCES (330 G) BUCKWHEAT FLOUR

1 TEASPOON SALT

0.71 OUNCES (20 G) PSYLLIUM SEED HUSKS

FLAX SEEDS TO SPRINKLE OVER THE ROLLS

Scout Bread

This bread really goes well with dessert cheeses. The nuttiness cuts the sweetness of the apricots and raisins, creating a good flavor combination to enhance the taste of the cheese.

- Blend all the ingredients to form a smooth dough.
- Cover the bowl with plastic wrap and let rise for 1½ hours.
- Turn the dough out onto a floured board.
- Oil your hands and shape dough into a round loaf. Place on a baking sheet covered with baking parchment. Sprinkle buckwheat flour over the loaf.
- Let bread rise for about 1 hour.
- Heat oven to 400°F. Bake bread for 45 minutes.

MAKES 1 LOAF
14.11 (400 G) BUTTERMILK
0.42 (12 G) YEAST
0.71 OUNCES (20 G) BUCK-
    WHEAT FLAKES
7.05 OUNCES (200 G) BUCK-
    WHEAT FLOUR
0.71 OUNCES (20 G) SYRUP
2.82 OUNCES (80 G) UNSUL-
    PHERED ORGANIC APRICOTS
1.41 OUNCES (40 G) WALNUTS
1.41 OUNCES (40 G) HAZEL-
    NUTS (FILBERTS)
1.76 OUNCES (50 G) RAISINS
½ TEASPOON SALT
0.35 OUNCES (10 G) PSYLLI-
    UM SEED HUSKS
CANOLA OIL FOR PAN
BUCKWHEAT FLOUR FOR WORK
    SURFACE
BUCKWHEAT FLOUR TO SPRIN-
    KLE OVER THE BREAD

Gratinéed Pears
with Blue Cheese

Fried in butter and gratinéed with cheese,
that is to say it is as good as it gets,
either for dessert or an appetizer.

- Heat oven to 450°F.
- Slice the pear into 8 slices, removing the seed pit.
- In a frying pan, on medium heat, fry the bread and pear slices in butter until golden.
- Move the bread to an ovenproof pan. Top with the pear slices and crumble the blue cheese on top.
- Gratinée in the oven for about 5 minutes until the cheese begins to melt.
- Drizzle with balsamic vinegar and serve.

MAKES 2 SERVINGS

1 PEAR
2 SLICES SCOUT BREAD
  (SEE PAGE 46)
1.76 OUNCES (50 G)
  BUTTER
1.76 OUNCES (50 G)
  BLUE CHEESE
1½ TABLESPOONS GOOD
  QUALITY BALSAMIC
  VINEGAR

The Danish

Here's a gluten-free version of the classic Danish rye bread that has good consistency and character. It is perfect for sandwiches and, for example, an accompaniment to meatballs and red beet salad.

- Whisk the yeast and water together.
- Add the remaining ingredients and blend to a smooth dough.
- Butter the bread pan (1½ quart) and pour in the dough.
- Flatten the dough on top and sprinkle with buckwheat flour.
- Let rise in the pan for about 1½ hours.
- Heat oven to 350°F and bake for 75 minutes.
- Cool bread completely, preferably waiting until the next day, before cutting.

MAKES 1 LOAF

0.71 OUNCES (20 G) YEAST

24.69 OUNCES (700 G) WATER

3.53 OUNCES (100 G) SUNFLOWER SEEDS

2.12 OUNCES (60 G) FLAX-SEEDS

2.12 OUNCES (60 G) SYRUP

0.71 OUNCES (20 G) ROSE-HIP POWDER

1.41 OUNCES (40 G) WHOLE BLACK PSYLLIUM SEEDS

½ TEASPOON BREAD SPICES

½ TEASPOON CUMIN

1 TEASPOON SALT

3.17 OUNCES (90 G) BROWN RICE FLOUR

4.23 OUNCES (120 G) BUCKWHEAT FLOUR

2.12 OUNCES (60 G) CORN-MEAL

1.06 OUNCES (30 G) PSYL-LIUM SEED HUSKS

BUTTER FOR THE PAN

BUCKWHEAT FLOUR TO SPRIN-KLE OVER THE BREAD

Meatballs

This is a super easy and excellent basic recipe for gluten-free meatballs.

- Whisk the egg, cornmeal, cream, onion powder, white pepper, and salt together.
- Blend in the ground beef and mix until even.
- Roll out small meatballs.
- Fry meatballs in a buttered pan on medium heat until they are cooked through.

MAKES 1 BATCH

1 EGG

1.69 OUNCES (1/2 DL) CORNMEAL

3.38 OUNCES (1 DL) WHIPPING CREAM

1 TABLESPOON ONION POWDER

1 TEASPOON WHITE PEPPER

1 TEASPOON SALT

17.64 OUNCES (500 G) GROUND BEEF

BUTTER FOR THE FRYING PAN

Red Beet Salad

Red beets are not just a pretty color but they also are amazingly tasty. We always make homemade red beet salad at Christmastime. This is our best recipe for it.

- Chop the beets and apple into small cubes.
- Finely chop the onion.
- Grate the horseradish.
- Blend the crème fraiche, mayonnaise, red beets, apple, onion, and horseradish.
- Taste and serve over a slice of good bread; top with warm meatballs.

MAKES 1 PORTION

14.11 OUNCES (400 G) PICKLED BEETS, WEIGHT WHEN DRAINED

½ SWEDISH APPLE

½ YELLOW ONION

2 TEASPOONS FRESH HORSERADISH

3.38 OUNCES (1 DL) CRÈME FRAICHE

3.38 OUNCES (1 DL) HOMEMADE MAYONNAISE (SEE PAGE 121)

Christmas Bread

A bread flavored with Christmas spices to bring out your Christmas spirit. Moist and soft in consistency, it is an excellent choice for the breakfast table during the Christmas holidays.

- Mix all the ingredients except for the psyllium seed husks into a smooth dough.
- Add the psyllium seed husks, stirring continually to prevent clumping.
- Cover the bowl with plastic wrap and let the dough rise for 2 hours
- Heat oven to 350°F.
- Turn dough out onto a floured surface and shape into a round loaf; sprinkle with buckwheat flour and place on baking sheet covered in backing parchment.
- After shaping, bake bread for 45 minutes.
- Cool bread completely before cutting.

MAKES 1 LOAF

17.64 OUNCES (500 G) MILK

0.71 OUNCES (20 G) YEAST

3.53 OUNCES (100 G) DARK SYRUP

10.58 OUNCES (300 G) BUCKWHEAT FLOUR

1.76 OUNCES (50 G) CORN-STARCH

1½ TEASPOONS SALT

2 TEASPOONS GROUND CLOVES

1 TEASPOON GINGER

3 TEASPOONS SEVILLE BITTER ORANGE

3 TEASPOONS BREAD SPICES

1.41 OUNCES (40 G) PSYLLIUM SEED HUSKS

BUCKWHEAT FLOUR FOR WORK SURFACE

BUCKWHEAT FLOUR TO SPRINKLE OVER THE BREAD

Special Christmas Bread

This bread is loaded with flavor! The bitterness of the Seville orange peel balances the sweetness of the candied peel and sultana raisins. Dried lingonberries plump up the bread and, with the added Christmas spices, this becomes a very flavorful loaf.

- Put orange peel in a bowl and completely cover with boiling water. Soak until peel is soft.
- Blend all the ingredients, except for the candied peel, raisins, orange peel, and fiber husks. Mix until dough is smooth.
- Chop the orange peel into small pieces.
- Carefully blend in the candied peel, raisins, and orange peel so the dough remains intact.
- Stir continually as you add the fiber husks to avoid clumping.
- Cover the bowl with plastic wrap and let the dough rise for 2 hours.
- Heat oven to 350°F.
- Turn dough out onto floured surface and shape into a round loaf. Sprinkle with buckwheat flour. Place loaf into a buttered pan.
- Bake for 45 minutes.
- Cool bread completely before cutting.

MAKES 1 LOAF

- 0.53 OUNCES (15 G) WHOLE SEVILLE BITTER ORANGE PEEL (1 PACKAGE)
- 17.64 OUNCES (500 G) COLD MILK
- 0.71 OUNCES (20 G) YEAST
- 4.23 OUNCES (120 G) DARK SYRUP
- 2.12 OUNCES (60 G) SWEETENED DRIED LINGONBERRIES
- 1.06 OUNCES (30 G) CORNSTARCH
- 12.35 OUNCES (350 G) BUCKWHEAT FLOUR
- 3 TEASPOONS GROUND CLOVES
- 2 TEASPOONS GINGER
- 1½ TEASPOONS SALT
- 2 TEASPOONS BREAD SPICES
- 0.71 OUNCES (20 G) CANDIED PEEL
- 1.76 OUNCES (50 G) SULTANA RAISINS
- 1.76 OUNCES (50 G) FIBER HUSKS
- BUCKWHEAT FLOUR FOR WORK SURFACE
- BUCKWHEAT FLOUR TO SPRINKLE OVER THE BREAD

Sunflower Rolls

*Small rolls filled with the goodness of
sunflower seeds. They can be served at any
occasion - picnics, the breakfast table,
or a buffet.*

- Dissolve the yeast in the water in a bowl.
- Blend in remaining ingredients.
- Cover bowl with plastic wrap and let dough
  rise for about 1½ hours.
- Shape the dough into 12 round rolls. Oil
  your hands to make it easier to handle the
  dough and lay the rolls on a baking sheet
  covered with baking parchment.
- Flatten the rolls slightly and sprinkle them
  with buckwheat flour.
- Let the rolls rise on the baking sheet for 1
  hour.
- Heat oven to 435°F. Bake rolls for 20
  minutes.

MAKES 12 ROLLS

21.16 OUNCES (600 G)
  WATER

0.88 OUNCES (25 G)
  YEAST

3.53 OUNCES (100 G)
  CORNSTARCH

3.53 OUNCES (100 G) SOY
  FLOUR

5.64 OUNCES (160 G)
  BUCKWHEAT FLOUR

1.41 (40 G) RICE FLOUR

1 TEASPOON SALT

1.41 (40 G) PSYLLIUM
  SEED HUSKS

1.76 OUNCES (50 G)
  SUNFLOWER SEEDS

BUCKWHEAT FLOUR FOR
  WORK SURFACE

The Sultan

This bread is chock-full of good ingredients. It is perfect as a breakfast bread, on a cheese board, or to revive your energy after a workout.

Step 1

- Weigh the polenta, black psyllium seeds, sunflower seeds, pumpkin seeds, and chia seeds.
- Bring the water to boil and pour it over the seeds. Cover the bowl with plastic wrap and let stand for 5 hours.

Step 2

- Add the rest of the ingredients except for the raisins and mix until dough is smooth.
- Stir in the raisins.
- Cover the bowl with plastic wrap and let rise for about 3 hours.
- Butter a 1-quart baking pan with canola oil and pour dough into it.
- Dampen your hands with water and lightly flatten the dough into the pan.
- Sprinkle a little buckwheat flour over the loaf.
- Let the bread rise until it reaches the edge of the pan. That should take about 1½ hours.
- Heat oven to 350°F. Bake bread for about 60 minutes.
- Cool bread completely (preferably until the next day) before cutting.

MAKES 1 LOAF

SOFTENING THE SEEDS, STEP 1
2.65 OUNCES (75 G) POLENTA
0.71 OUNCES (20 G) BLACK PSYLLIUM SEEDS
2.12 OUNCES (60 G) SUNFLOWER SEEDS
3.53 OUNCES (100 G) PUMPKIN SEEDS
0.53 OUNCES (15 G) CHIA SEEDS
18.52 OUNCES (525 G) BOILING WATER

STEP 2
2.65 OUNCES (75 G) SYRUP
0.71 OUNCES (20 G) YEAST
1 EGG
1 TEASPOON SALT
2.12 OUNCES (60 G) POTATO FLOUR
5.29 OUNCES (150 G) BUCKWHEAT FLOUR
0.35 OUNCES (10 G) FIBER HUSKS
5.29 OUNCES (150 G) SULTANA RAISINS

TIP!
If you can't find sultana raisins in your local grocery store, use regular and/or golden raisins instead.

Coarse Rolls

These tasty rolls are crusty, chewy, and sweet. They are perfect for breakfast and they freeze well.

- Mix all the ingredients until dough is smooth.
- Cover the bowl with plastic wrap and let rise for about 2 hours.
- Sprinkle work surface with buckwheat flour. Oil your hands and a spoon. Use the spoon to divide the dough into 10 equal-sized pieces and roll each out into a round bun.
- Cover the baking sheet with baking parchment and place rolls on pan.
- Let rise for about 40 minutes.
- Heat oven to 435°F. Bake roll for 20-25 minutes.

MAKES 10 ROLLS

17.64 OUNCES (500 G) MILK

0.71 OUNCES (20 G) YEAST

0.88 OUNCES (25 G) CANOLA OIL

1.76 OUNCES (50 G) DARK SYRUP

0.88 OUNCES (25 G) FIBREX

0.35 OUNCES (10 G) WHOLE BLACK PSYLLIUM SEEDS

3.53 OUNCES (100 G) ROLLED OATS

2.47 OUNCES (70 G) BUCK-WHEAT FLOUR

0.88 OUNCES (25 G) SOY FLOUR

¼ TEASPOON BREAD SPICES

1 TEASPOON SALT

0.71 OUNCES (20) G PSYL-LIUM SEED HUSKS

CANOLA OIL FOR HANDS

BUCKWHEAT FLOUR FOR WORK SURFACE

Thin Bread

This moist and very tasty thin bread can be cooked either in a dry skillet on the stovetop or on a baking sheet in the oven. Roll the dough out with a knobbly rolling pin so that the bread doesn't rise too much when baking.

- Whisk the yeast into the cold milk.
- Add the remaining ingredients and work to an even dough.
- Cover the bowl with plastic wrap and let rise for about 2 hours.
- Divide the dough into 8 equal-sized pieces.
- Sprinkle work surface with soy flour and roll out the dough into thin circles.
- Cook the bread in a dry skillet over medium heat or bake on a baking sheet in 400°F oven until they've taken on color on both sides and feel light.
- Stack the breads and cover them with a tea towel so they don't dry out.

MAKES 8 PIECES
0.42 OUNCES (12 G) YEAST
14.11 (400 G) COLD MILK
0.71 OUNCES (20 G) LIGHT SYRUP
½ TEASPOON SALT
2.12 OUNCES (60 G) SOY FLOUR
3.53 OUNCES (100 G) OAT FLOUR
0.71 OUNCES (20 G) FIBER HUSKS
SOY FLOUR FOR WORK SURFACE

cellar French Rolls

Authentic cellar French rolls are left to rise in a cellar, but, since not every home has one, we offer an easier variation. These are just as good and moist, perfect for Sunday lunch, weekend breakfast or for our steak sandwich (see page 68).

- Whisk all the ingredients until blended to a smooth dough.
- Cover the bowl with plastic wrap and let rise for 1½ hours.
- Heat oven to 435°F.
- Flour work surface with rice flour, oil your hands with canola oil and turn dough out onto work surface.
- Pull the dough out to a rectangle about 15¾ x 8 inches.
- Fold the dough double lengthwise and cut into 8 equal-sized pieces using a dough scraper or knife.
- Place the rolls on a baking sheet covered with baking parchment. Sprinkle rolls with a little rice flour.
- Bake the rolls for 20 minutes.
- Cool rolls completely before eating.

MAKES 8 SMALL ROLLS

17.64 OUNCES (500 G) WATER

0.35 OUNCES (10 G) HONEY

0.71 OUNCES (20 G) YEAST

2.47 OUNCES (70 G) CORNMEAL

4.23 OUNCES (120 G) RICE FLOUR

6 OUNCES (170 G) BUCK-WHEAT FLOUR

1 TEASPOON SALT

0.35 OUNCES (10 G) FIBER HUSKS

RICE FLOUR FOR WORK SURFACE

CANOLA OIL FOR HANDS

RICE FLOUR TO SPRINKLE OVER THE ROLLS

Steak Sandwich

A big serving with all the extras! It's
perfect for brunch and just right with a cold
beer.

- Fry the bacon over medium heat until crispy. Lay on paper towels to soak up excess oil.
- Slice the tomatoes and rinse the lettuce.
- Salt and pepper the meat.
- Turn on the stove burner to high and heat up a frying pan.
- Melt the butter in the pan. When the butter has "quieted down," add the meat.
- Fry the meat for a few minutes on each side, depending on thickness. We like meat to be pink all the way through.
- Let the meat set for a couple of minutes on a cutting board.
- Toast the bread in a toaster.
- Lightly rub the garlic clove into the rolls.
- Cut the meat finely and spread over the rolls.
- Layer the béarnaise sauce, tomato slices, lettuce, and finely chopped parsley on top. Top with bacon.
- Serve immediately accompanied by a gluten-free beer if you like.

MAKES 2 SERVINGS
2 CELLAR FRENCH ROLLS
   (SEE PAGE 67)
4.94 OUNCES (40 G)
   BACON
2 TOMATOES
A FEW LETTUCE LEAVES
7.05 OUNCES (200 G)
   SWEDISH BEEF OR
   ENTRECÔTE
SALT
PEPPER
2 TABLESPOONS BUTTER
   FOR FRYING
1 GARLIC CLOVE
BÉARNAISE SAUCE (SEE
   PAGE 120)
2 SPRIGS OF PARSLEY

Oat Crisp Bread

Thin and crunchy crisp bread with the great taste of oats. It can be served for breakfast or parties. Why not make a tasty little snack with our butter bean cream (see page 131)!

- Whisk all the ingredients to a smooth dough.
- Cover the bowl with plastic wrap and let rise for about 1½ hours.
- Divide the dough into 4 equal-sized pieces.
- Sprinkle the work surface with buckwheat flour. Roll each piece of dough into a thin circle, about 9¾ inches in diameter. If possible use a knobbly rolling pin.
- Heat oven to 400°F. Bake the crisp breads immediately, one at a time, for about 15 minutes each on a baking sheet with parchment.
- Cool the bread on a cooling rack.

MAKES 4 ROUND BREADS

10.58 OUNCES (300 G) COLD WATER

0.35 OUNCES (10 G) YEAST

4.23 OUNCES (120 G) OAT FLOUR

0.88 OUNCES (25 G) CORNSTARCH

0.35 OUNCES (10 G) SYRUP

1.41 OUNCES (40 G) BUCKWHEAT FLOUR

1.06 OUNCES (30 G) ROLLED OATS

¼ TEASPOON BREAD SPICES

1 TEASPOON ROSEHIP POWDER

½ TEASPOON SLAT

0.35 OUNCES (10 G) FIBER HUSKS

BUCKWHEAT FLOUR FOR WORK SURFACE

Corn Muffins

Delicious yellow corn muffins that can be served with soup or for a taco buffet. You can prepare the muffins at the last minute because they are quick-baking, non-yeast rolls.

- Heat oven to 435°F.
- Mix the water, egg, and olive oil in a bowl.
- Add the cornmeal, baking powder, salt, and psyllium seed husks.
- Let the dough rest for about 15 minutes.
- Divide the dough into 8 muffin cups placed in a muffin pan.
- Bake for 20 minutes in the center of the oven.

MAKES 8 MUFFINS

12.35 OUNCES (350 G) COLD WATER

1 EGG

1.41 OUNCES (40 G) OLIVE OIL

3.53 OUNCES (100 G) CORNMEAL

1 TEASPOON BAKING POWDER

½ TEASPOON SALT

0.53 OUNCES (15 G) PSYLLIUM SEED HUSKS

8 MUFFIN CUPS

Tortillas

Tacos have become almost every Swedish family's favorite Friday night meal. These easily prepared tortillas can also be used for wrap sandwiches to take on an outing.

- Mix all the ingredients to a smooth dough.
- Let dough rest for 15 minutes.
- Divide the dough into 10 pieces. Sprinkle work surface with cornmeal and roll out tortillas to thin rounds.
- Cook the tortillas one at a time in a dry skillet over high heat until lightly browned on each side and it feels light.
- Stack the tortillas on a plate and cover with a tea towel to prevent them from drying out.

MAKES 10 TORTILLAS

14.11 OUNCES (400 G) COLD WATER

1 TEASPOON BAKING POWDER

1.76 OUNCES (50 G) RICE FLOUR

5.29 OUNCES (150 G) CORNMEAL

½ TEASPOON SALT

1.06 OUNCES (30 G) FIBER HUSKS

CORNMEAL FOR WORK SURFACE

Creamy Bean Dip

Creamy, soft dip for the taco buffet or lunch sandwiches with veggies and mature cheese.

- If using canned beans, rinse them well in cold water.
- Chop the onion finely.
- Grate the garlic.
- Sauté the onion and garlic in the oil until translucent. Remove from the heat and add the chocolate. Stir until chocolate melts.
- Mix the chili flakes with the onion mix, beans, and vinegar.
- Process in a blender until smooth. Salt to taste.

<u>MAKES 1 SERVING</u>

14.11 OUNCES (400 G) BLACK BEANS, COOKED

1 YELLOW ONION

2 GARLIC CLOVES

OIL

1 SQUARE DARK CHOCOLATE, 70%

1 TEASPOON CHILI FLAKES

½ TEASPOON WHITE WINE VINEGAR

SALT

Taco-Spiced Ground Beef

It's super easy to make your own taco spice mix. You can avoid any unwanted additives and vary the flavor to your taste.

- Brown the meat on high heat, stirring in all the spices.
- Halve the lime and squeeze juice of each half over the meat; add the tomato purée, water, and stock.
- Simmer mixture for 3-4 minutes.

<u>MAKES 1 SERVING</u>

21.16 OUNCES (600 G) GROUND MEAT

5 TEASPOONS CUMIN

1 TEASPOON CHILI FLAKES

2 TEASPOONS OREGANO

¼ TEASPOON BLACK PEPPER

1 TEASPOON BROWN SUGAR

1 TEASPOON SALT

1 TEASPOON COCOA

1 LIME

1 TABLESPOON TOMATO PURÉE

¼ CUP WATER

2 TABLESPOONS CONCENTRATED VEAL STOCK

Oatcakes

Thin cakes with a wonderful flavor from the combination of oats, buckwheat, and honey. They are extra tasty just out of the oven spread with butter.

- Mix the yeast, butter, and honey to an even batter.
- Whisk in the milk until the dough is free of lumps.
- Add the buckwheat flour, rolled oats, salt, baking powder, and psyllium seed husks.
- Cover the bowl with plastic wrap and let dough rise for 2 hours.
- Divide the dough into 8 pieces. Spread the pieces on baking sheets covered with baking parchment – 4 oatcakes per sheet.
- Oil a spatula and flatten out each cake until about 4¾ inches in diameter.
- Let the cakes rise on the baking sheets for about 1 hour.
- Heat oven to 435°F.
- Bake oatcakes for about 15 minutes.

MAKES 8 CAKES

0.71 OUNCES (20 G)
  YEAST

0.88 OUNCES (25 G)
  BUTTER, ROOM TEMPERA-
  TURE

1.41 OUNCES (40 G)
  HONEY

17.64 OUNCES (500 G)
  MILK

7.05 OUNCES (200 G)
  BUCKWHEAT FLOUR

3.53 OUNCES (100 G)
  ROLLED OATS

½ TEASPOON SALT

1 TEASPOON BAKING
  POWDER

0.71 OUNCES (20 G)
  PSYLLIUM SEED HUSKS

Seed Rolls

Chia seeds are chock-full of omega-3, antioxidants, and calcium so these rolls aren't just light and tasty, they give your body a mass of nutrition into the bargain.

MAKES 10 ROLLS
27.16 OUNCES (770 G) WATER
0.71 OUNCES (20 G) YEAST
0.35 OUNCES (10 G) CHIA SEEDS
0.35 OUNCES (10 G) WHOLE BLACK PSYLLIUM SEEDS
0.35 OUNCES (10 G) CORNSTARCH
8.82 OUNCES (250 G) CORNMEAL
2.47 OUNCES (70 G) ROLLED OATS
1 TEASPOON SALT
0.53 OUNCES (15 G) PSYLLIUM SEED HUSKS

- Whisk together the water, yeast, chia seeds, psyllium seeds, and cornstarch.
- Add the cornmeal, rolled oats, salt, and psyllium seed husks.
- Cover the bowl with plastic wrap and let dough rise for about 2 hours.
- Use two spoons to form 10 rolls, dividing them onto two baking sheets covered with baking parchment paper.
- Let the rolls rise on the baking sheets for about 30 minutes.
- Heat oven to 435°F.
- Bake rolls in center of oven for 25 minutes.
- Cool rolls completely before cutting them.

Buckwheat Rolls

Perfect, light rolls that will keep fresh for several days. They are equally good for breakfast or picnic sandwiches. They have a mild, slightly nutty flavor.

- Coarsely chop the pumpkin seeds.
- Dissolve the yeast in the water, whisking them together in a bowl or stand mixer.
- Add the psyllium seed husks.
- Add the buckwheat flour, pumpkin seeds, and salt to the dough.
- Cover the bowl with plastic wrap and let dough rise for about 2 hours.
- Use two spoons to form 10 rolls, dividing them onto two baking sheets covered with baking parchment.
- Sprinkle the rolls with buckwheat flour and let them rise on the pans for 30 minutes.
- Heat oven to 400°F. Bake rolls for 25 minutes.
- Cool rolls completely before cutting.

MAKES 10 ROLLS

2.12 OUNCES (60 G) PUMPKIN SEEDS

27.16 OUNCES (770 G) WATER

0.71 OUNCES (20 G) YEAST

0.88 OUNCES (25 G) PSYLLIUM SEED HUSKS

9.17 OUNCES (260 G) BUCKWHEAT FLOUR

1 TEASPOON SALT

BUCKWHEAT FLOUR TO SPRINKLE OVER THE ROLLS

Picnic Buns
with Chicken and Bacon

These buns are particularly good for the picnic basket. We haven't stinted on anything so you are guaranteed to be full and happy. Make sure the chicken and bacon you choose are the best quality.

- Sliver the chicken fillet and mix with the curry and salt.
- Fry the chicken in the butter over high heat until browned.
- Add the mango chutney to the frying pan and let it cook down with the chicken until the mixture is slightly gelatinous and shiny. Set aside until time to serve.
- Fry the bacon until crispy and then place on paper towels to absorb excess oil.
- Grate or press the garlic into a bowl and mix with the mayonnaise and crème fraiche. Refrigerate until ready to serve.
- Thinly slice the onion and tomato.
- Cut open each bun. Spread garlic dressing on each side. Fill the buns with lettuce, tomato, onion, chicken, and bacon. Pack into the picnic basket or enjoy as is.

MAKES 4 ROLLS
10.58 OUNCES (300 G) CHICKEN FILLET
1 TABLESPOON CURRY
½ TEASPOON SALT
1 TABLESPOON BUTTER
1.69 OUNCES (1/2 DL) MANGO CHUTNEY
8 SLICES OF BACON
1 GARLIC CLOVE
1.69 OUNCES (1/2 DL) MAYONNAISE (SEE PAGE 121)
1.69 OUNCES (1/2 DL) CRÈME FRAICHE
½ WHITE ONION
1 TOMATO
4 BUCKWHEAT ROLLS (SEE PAGE 85)
4 LEAVES OF HEAD LETTUCE

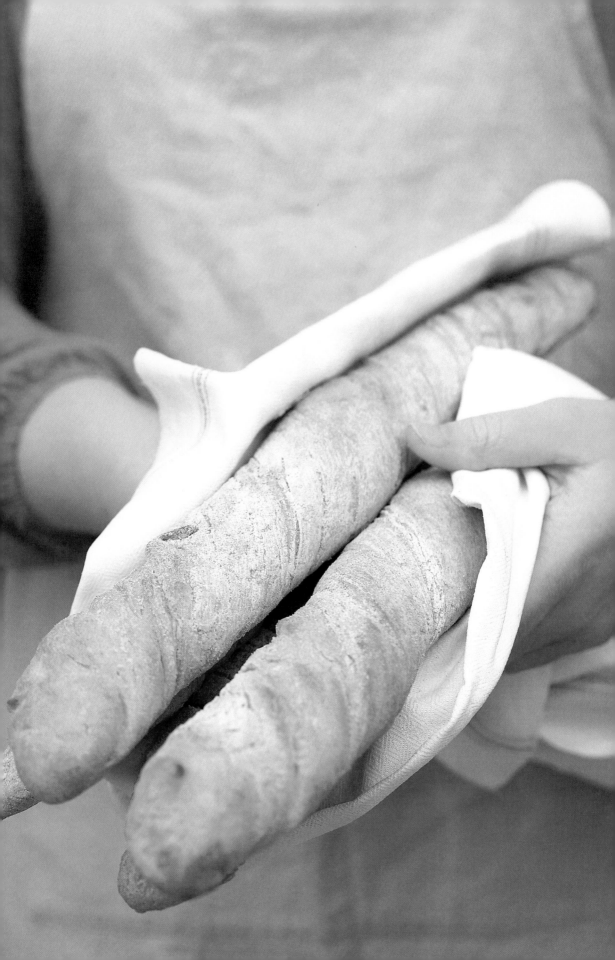

Baguettes

Baguettes are the king of the bread world with their fine crust and moist crumb. They are perfect for any occasion: breakfast, in the picnic basket, on the cheese board, or holiday meals.

- Blend all the ingredients in a stand mixer for 5 minutes until the dough is even but loose.
- Cover the bowl with plastic wrap and let dough rise for 2 hours.
- Heat oven to 435°F.
- Oil your hands. Sprinkle buckwheat flour on work surface and turn dough out onto surface.
- Divide the dough into two pieces and shape each into a baguette. Dust with buckwheat flour and twist dough several times for a rustic look.
- Place the baguettes on a baking sheet covered with baking parchment.
- Bake for 30-35 minutes.

<u>MAKES 2 BAGUETTES</u>

17.64 OUNCES (500 G) WATER

0.71 OUNCES (20 G) YEAST

1 TEASPOON SALT

2.82 OUNCES (80 G) CORNMEAL

5.29 OUNCES (150 G) RICE FLOUR

5.29 OUNCES (150 G) BUCKWHEAT FLOUR

0.53 OUNCES (15 G) FIBER HUSKS

CANOLA OIL FOR YOUR HANDS

BUCKWHEAT FLOUR FOR WORK SURFACE

Chocolate Hazelnut Spread

Sinfully good on toast. Maybe not the world's healthiest spread but it is homemade with all natural ingredients. It will make the perfect impression at a Sunday brunch.

- Toast the hazelnuts in a skillet over high heat until they brown slightly and the husks start to loosen.
- Place the nuts in one half of a clean tea towel and fold the other half over them. Rub the nuts around to completely loosen the husks.
- Process the nuts in a blender to an even paste. Add the butter, sugar, and salt. Process a little more until the mixture is completely blended.
- Heat the cream on the stovetop while you chop the chocolate finely. Mix the chocolate into the cream and remove pot from stove.
- Blend the chocolate with the hazelnut mix to a smooth cream. Pour mixture into a clean glass jar.
- Store in the refrigerator.

MAKES 1 PORTION
5.29 OUNCES (150 G) HAZELNUTS
1.76 OUNCES (50 G) BUTTER
1.69 OUNCES (1/2 DL) SUGAR
¼ TEASPOON SALT
6.76 OUNCES (2 DL) WHIPPING CREAM
3.53 OUNCES (100 G) DARK CHOCOLATE, 50-60%

French Loaf

The classic French loaf is an important basic recipe that can be used for sandwich tart, poor knights, and toast for breakfast. Our recipe for French bread is moist, long-lasting, and gluten-free.

- Whisk the yeast in the water to dissolve.
- Mix in the cornmeal, rice flour, buckwheat flour, and salt.
- Add the fiber husks while mixing vigorously to prevent clumping.
- Butter a 1½-quart bread pan.
- Turn the dough into the pan and cover with poppy seeds.
- Let the dough rise for about 1 hour.
- Heat oven to 400°F. Bake bread for 1 hour.
- Cool bread completely before cutting.

<u>MAKES 1 LOAF</u>

0.53 OUNCES (15 G) YEAST

29.98 OUNCES (850 G) WATER

3 OUNCES (85 G) CORNMEAL

6 OUNCES (170 G) RICE FLOUR

9.17 OUNCES (260 G) BUCKWHEAT FLOUR

1 TEASPOON SALT

0.71 OUNCES (20 G) FIBER HUSKS

BUTTER FOR THE BAKING PAN

POPPY SEEDS TO SPRINKLE OVER THE BREAD

Sandwich Tart

Sandwich tarts are classic for parties, christen-
ings, or student festivities. Try our scrumptious
sandwich the next time you invite friends for a
party. We - like many others - love the flavors
from the Italian kitchen and here we've combined
some of our favorites.

- Toast the pine nuts in a dry skillet until slightly browned.
- Thinly slice the zucchini lengthwise with a cheese grater or mandolin.
- Fry the zucchini until soft in the olive oil over medium heat. Put into a bowl and let cool.

Tomato Paste

- Process the sun-dried tomatoes, basil, balsamic vinegar, cream, and black pepper in a blender. The paste doesn't have to be completely smooth - it is nice to have some chunks in the paste.

Ricotta Cream

- Blend the ricotta cheese and olive oil with a little salt and black pepper.

Toppings

- Cut the loaf of bread into four lengthwise layers; trim away the crust.
- Spread tomato paste, ham, parmesan cheese, and zucchini on the first layer. Add the next layer of bread and repeat the fillings. Do the same with the third layer of bread. Finish with the fourth layer of bread, which does not have any filling.
- Spread the ricotta cream evenly over the entire tart.
- Surround the edges with the air-dried ham.
- Top with arugula, basil leaves, and pine nuts.
- Drizzle tart with a little olive oil just before serving.

MAKES 1 SANDWICH TART
1 LOAF FRENCH BREAD (SEE PAGE 93)
1.41 OUNCES (40 G) PINE NUTS
1 ZUCCHINI
OLIVE OIL

TOMATO PASTE
60 G SUN-DRIED TOMATOES
½ PACKAGE FRESH BASIL
1 TEASPOON BALSAMIC VINEGAR
5.07 OUNCES (1 1/2 DL) WHIPPING CREAM
½ TEASPOON BLACK PEPPER

RICOTTA CREAM
8.82 OUNCES (250 G) RICOTTA CHEESE
2 TABLESPOONS OLIVE OIL
SALT
BLACK PEPPER

TOPPINGS
4.94 OUNCES (140 G) AIR-DRIED HAM
3.38 OUNCES (1 DL) GRATED PARMESAN CHEESE
2.47 OUNCES (70 G) ARUGULA
½ PACKAGE FRESH BASIL

Open-faced Sandwiches

A classic sandwich tart in the form of open-faced sandwiches that can be served at any festivity or party in the spring or summer. Make your own mayonnaise (see page 121) so the fillings will have a good basic flavor.

Shrimp Filling
- Peel the shrimp and coarsely chop.
- Flavor mayonnaise with lemon juice to taste.
- Finely chop the onion.
- Mix all the ingredients and fold in the shrimp.
- Salt and pepper to taste.

Caviar Filling
- Whip the cream and crème fraiche together until firm.
- Fold in the mayonnaise, caviar, and dill.
- Salt and pepper to taste.

Toppings
- Place each of the 4 slices of bread on a separate plate.
- For each sandwich:
- Spread the shrimp filling over the bread and top with another slice of bread.
- Spread half of the caviar filling over the bread and top with another bread layer.
- Spread the rest of the caviar filling over the entire sandwich.
- Decorate each of the sandwiches with the toppings.

MAKES 4 SANDWICHES
12 SLICES FRENCH LOAF
  (SEE PAGE 93)

SHRIMP FILLING
8.82 OUNCES (250 G)
  UNPEELED SHRIMP
3.38 OUNCES (1 DL)
  MAYONNAISE (SEE PAGE 121)
LEMON JUICE TO TASTE
1 QUART RED ONION
3.38 OUNCES (1 DL) CRÈME
  FRAICHE
1 TABLESPOON FINELY
  CHOPPED DILL
SALT AND PEPPER

CAVIAR FILLING
10.14 OUNCES (2 DL)
  WHIPPING CREAM
3.38 OUNCES (1 DL) CRÈME
  FRAICHE
1.69 OUNCES (1/2 DL)
  MAYONNAISE (SEE PAGE 121)
2 TABLESPOONS RED CAVIAR
1 TABLESPOON CHOPPED DILL
SALT AND PEPPER

TOPPINGS
1 CONTAINER CRISPY LETTUCE
CHERRY TOMATOES
8.82 OUNCES (250 G)
  PEELED SHRIMP
CUCUMBER
2 HARD BOILED EGGS
4 SLICES COLD SMOKED SALMON
RED CAVIAR
DILL
LEMON SLICES

croissants

A croissant isn't just any old bread – it is a crispy pleasure. Croissants can be frozen before or after baking. Frozen baked croissants only need a few minutes reheating at 435°F to restore their crispness. Croissants frozen before baking are baked for 30 minutes at 350°F. In any case, croissants are best right out of the oven! See more in the illustrated instructions on the following pages.

- Whisk the yeast into the milk.
- Mix in the baking powder, salt, sugar, cornstarch, rice flour, and soy flour until evenly blended.
- Sprinkle the fiber husks over the dough and mix in quickly.
- Cover the bowl with plastic wrap and let rise for about 2 hours.
- Sprinkle the work surface with rice flour. Roll the dough out to a rectangle 11¾ x 15¾ inches.
- Spread slivers of the cold butter over half of the rectangle.
- Fold the dough in half and pinch the edges together well so that the butter doesn't seep out.
- Carefully roll the dough into a rectangle. Try to keep the edges as straight as possible. As you work, sprinkle flour over the work surface and the dough to prevent sticking.
- Make the first three layers: fold one short side over two-thirds of the dough and then fold the other short side over the first fold so that you have 3 layers. Turn the dough 180°.
- Roll out the dough to the same size as the previous rectangle and fold as for a "business letter" as before.
- Roll out the dough the same way once more and fold.
- Roll the dough out into a rectangle about 8 x 15¾ inches.
- Cut the rectangle into 8 – 10 triangular pieces. Roll up each triangle from the widest edge up to the tip.
- Cover baking sheet with baking parchment. Place the croissants on baking sheet with tip of each pointing down.
- Let rise for 45 minutes.
- Heat oven to 350°F. Bake croissants for 30 minutes.

MAKES 8 – 10 CROISSANTS

0.35 OUNCES (10 G) YEAST
14.11 OUNCES (400 G) COLD MILK
½ TEASPOON BAKING POWDER
½ TEASPOON SALT
2 TABLESPOONS SUGAR
2.47 OUNCES (70 G) CORNSTARCH
2.12 OUNCES (60 G) RICE FLOUR
3.53 OUNCES (100 G) SOY FLOUR
1.06 (30 G) FIBER HUSKS

FOR ROLLING OUT
RICE FLOUR
5.29 OUNCES (150 G) COLD BUTTER

Roll the dough out to a rectangle 11¾ x 15¾ inches. Spread slivers of the cold butter over half of the rectangle.

Fold the dough in half and pinch the edges together well so that the butter doesn't seep out.

Fold the dough as for a letter into 3 layers. Roll the dough out once more to the same size rectangle as before; repeat the turn and rolling 2 more times.

Roll the dough out into a rectangle about 8 x 15¾ inches. Cut the rectangle into 8 - 10 triangular pieces.

Roll up each triangle from the widest edge up to the tip and place on baking sheet.

Plum Marmalade

Plum marmalade can be made with any type of plum. We used small red plums with yellow fruit. The taste and color of the marmalade will vary depending on the type of plum you use but they will all be equally good.

- Deseed the plums.
- Pour the sugar and plums into a heavy saucepan.
- Bring mixture to a boil and then simmer just below boiling until the sugar has dissolved and the plums are soft.
- Pour the marmalade into clean glass jars, seal the lid and set jars upside down until the mixture is cool.
- Store in the refrigerator.

MAKES 1 PORTION

21.16 OUNCES (600 G) PLUMS

14.11 OUNCES (400 G) SUGAR

TIP!

It is important that the jars are very clean. Wash and rinse them well or fill them with boiling water to kill all the bacteria. Fill the jars to the brim with marmalade, keeping in mind that the marmalade will be extremely hot as you pour. Place the lid on the jars immediately after filling to create a vacuum which will help preserve the marmalade longer.

Cherry Marmalade

When we make marmalade, we feel like we are preserving all the wonderful smells, colors, and flavors of summer. Maybe you'll experience the same feeling if you have a large cherry tree and can prepare the summer's most luxurious marmalade.

- Pour the sugar and cherries into a heavy saucepan and bring to a boil.
- Boil for about 10 minutes or until the cherries split.
- Let the mixture cool for a while and then pour it through a sieve. Use your fingers to remove the cherry pits, being careful not to burn your fingers.* Save the cherry meat and peel.
- Pour the marmalade back into the pot and bring to boil to kill any bacteria.
- Pour the marmalade into clean glass jars.

*We think this is the easiest way to remove the cherry pits. Of course, if you want, you can remove the pits before you cook the cherries and sugar.

MAKES 1 PORTION
21.16 OUNCES (600 G) CHERRIES WITH PITS IN
14.11 OUNCES (400 G) SUGAR

Tip!
It is important that the jars are very clean. Wash and rinse them well or fill them with boiling water to kill all the bacteria. Fill the jars to the brim with marmalade, keeping in mind that the marmalade will be extremely hot as you pour. Place the lid on the jars immediately after filling to create a vacuum which will help preserve the marmalade longer.

Chicken wraps

Absolutely delicious chicken wraps that can be endlessly varied. They are perfect for a picnic or lunch on the run.

- Mix the tortilla dough and set aside.
- Slice the chicken fillet, red pepper, and onion. Blend in the spices and rice flour and let mixture stand for at least 10 minutes.
- Divide the tortilla dough into 4 pieces. Sprinkle work surface with cornmeal and roll out dough for 4 large wraps.
- Bake the tortillas in a hot skillet for a few minutes on each side. Cover them with a clean tea towel until time to serve.
- Make the cheese sauce by heating the crème fraiche, cheese, and nutmeg on low heat until the cheese has melted.
- Fry the chicken mixture until the chicken is cooked through.
- Dice the avocados and tomatoes.
- Make the wraps by filling each tortilla with chicken, cheese sauce, and veggies. Top with jalapeño to taste. Don't overfill the wraps – you need to be able to wrap the tortillas around the fillings.
- The easiest way to fold a wrap is to leave some empty space along the bottom and sides of the tortilla. Fold up the bottom until it covers some of the chicken filling and then overlap the sides so that none of the fillings fall out.

MAKES 4 WRAPS
1 RECIPE TORTILLA DOUGH
(SEE PAGE 75)

CHICKEN FILLING
14.11 OUNCES (400 G)
  CHICKEN FILLET
1 RED BELL PEPPER
1 RED ONION
1 TEASPOON GROUND CORIAN-
DER
1 TEASPOON CUMIN
1 TEASPOON COCOA
1 TEASPOON SMOKED PAPRIKA
1 TEASPOON ONION POWDER
1 TEASPOON GARLIC POWDER
½ TEASPOON CAYENNE PEPPER
2 TEASPOONS SALT
1 TABLESPOON RICE FLOUR

CHEESE SAUCE
6.76 OUNCES (2 DL) CRÈME
  FRAICHE
5.29 OUNCES (150 G) GRATED
  CHEDDAR CHEESE
¼ TEASPOON GROUND NUTMEG

SERVING
1 PACKAGE CASCADE LETTUCE
  MIX
2 AVOCADOS
2 TOMATOES
3.38 OUNCES (1 DL) CHOPPED
  PICKLED JALAPEÑO

Lemon Curd

This is as good as it gets! Invite some friends for afternoon tea and serve them this delicious lemon curd with freshly baked scones, marmalade, cheese, and butter. Of course, you'll want to enjoy a nice cup of tea – our favorite is the classic Earl Grey.

- Wash the lemons well.
- Grate the lemon peel with a grater or zest grater.
- Squeeze the juice from the lemons.
- Mix the lemon peel and juice with the sugar and eggs in a saucepan.
- Heat mixture over low heat, stirring constantly until mixture has thickened. Remove pan from heat.
- Cut the cold butter into small cubes and add to lemon mixture, stirring continually.
- Once the butter has melted, the lemon curd is ready.
- Pour into a clean glass jar and store in refrigerator.

MAKES 1 PORTION
2 LEMONS
10.14 OUNCES (3 DL) SUGAR
2 EGGS
3.53 OUNCES (100 G) COLD BUTTER

TIP!
It is important that the jars are very clean. Wash and rinse them well or fill them with boiling water to kill all the bacteria. Fill the jars to the brim with lemon curd, keeping in mind that the curd will be extremely hot as you pour. Place the lid on the jars immediately after filling to create a vacuum which will help preserve the lemon curd longer.

Small Butter Rolls

Lovely little butter rolls for the tea table, breakfast, or instead of buns for an afternoon coffee break. The butter between the layers makes them extra delicious and they should be eaten fresh from the oven. Use butter and do not substitute margarine. See more in the illustrated instructions on the next two pages.

- Whisk the yeast into the milk.
- Blend in the remaining ingredients and mix to a smooth dough.
- Cover bowl with plastic wrap and let dough rise for 1½ hours.
- Sprinkle work surface with rice flour. Roll out dough to a rectangle approximately 11¾ x 15¾ inches. Lift the dough to make sure it isn't sticking.
- Mix the butter with the cornstarch and spread over the dough.
- Fold one long side two-thirds up and then fold the other side over it so the piece has 3 even layers.
- Cut the dough into 10 equal-sized pieces. Roll up each piece. Cover baking sheet with baking parchment. Place rolls on the pan with the cut side down.
- Spray or drizzle the rolls with water and sprinkle with poppy seeds.
- Let the rolls rise for about 30 minutes.
- Heat oven to 435°F. Bake rolls for 20 minutes.

MAKES 10 ROLLS

0.42 OUNCES (12 G) YEAST

17.64 OUNCES (500 G) COLD MILK

½ TEASPOON SALT

3.53 OUNCES (100 G) CORNMEAL

2.12 OUNCES (60 G) CORNSTARCH

6.17 OUNCES (175 G) BUCKWHEAT FLOUR

1 TABLESPOON SUGAR

0.71 OUNCES (20 G) FIBER HUSKS

1.76 OUNCES (50 G) BUTTER AT ROOM TEMPERATURE

1 TEASPOON CORNSTARCH

RICE FLOUR FOR WORK SURFACE

POPPY SEEDS FOR SPRIN-KLING OVER THE ROLLS

Roll out dough to a rectangle approximately 11¾ x 15¾ inches. Mix the butter with the cornstarch and spread over the dough.

Fold one long side two-thirds up and then fold the other side over it so the piece has 3 even layers.

Cut the dough into 10 equal-sized pieces. Roll up each piece. Cover baking sheet with baking parchment. Place rolls on the pan with the cut side down.

Spray or drizzle the rolls with water and sprinkle with poppy seeds before baking them in the oven

Scones

Scones are at their best served freshly baked with marmalade and lemon curd. They are excellent with evening coffee or for a weekend breakfast. They are also quick and easy to bake.

- Heat oven to 435°F.
- Mix the soy flour, rice flour, psyllium seed husks, raw sugar, baking powder, and salt in a bowl.
- Add the butter and mix until dough is evenly blended.
- Blend in the milk.
- Let dough rest for 15 minutes.
- Spoon out 10 pieces onto a baking sheet covered with baking parchment.
- Bake for 15 minutes on center rack of oven.

MAKES 10 SCONES

4.23 OUNCES (120 G) SOY FLOUR

4.23 OUNCES (120 G) RICE FLOUR

0.28 OUNCES (8 G) PSYLLIUM SEED HUSKS

½ TABLESPOON UNREFINED SUGAR

2 TEASPOONS BAKING POWDER

¼ TEASPOON SALT

2.82 OUNCES (80 G) BUTTER

17.64 OUNCES (500 G) MILK

Black Currant Marmalade

Black currants are our favorites. Their full flavor is indicated by the dramatically dark purple color of the berries. If you can't manage to make the marmalade during your summer holidays when the currants are ripe, pick them and store them in the freezer — then you'll have tasty marmalade all year.

- Pour the currants and sugar into a heavy saucepan.
- Bring mixture to a boil and let simmer until the sugar has dissolved and the currants are soft.
- Pour the marmalade into clean glass jars (see Tips on page 104 for how to prepare jars); close the lid and store upside down until the marmalade is cool. Store in refrigerator.

MAKES 1 PORTION

28.22 OUNCES (800 G) RINSED BLACK CURRANTS

2.2 LBS SUGAR

114

Hamburger Buns

Good, light hamburger buns that are easy to bake. You can fill the buns with our good hamburgers (see page 118) made with prime rib and smoked chili dressing or your own favorite hamburger.

- Mix all the ingredients together.
- Cover the bowl with plastic wrap and let dough rise for about 1½ hours.
- Oil your hands to make it easier to handle the dough and then shape the dough into 6 round rolls. Place the buns on a baking sheet covered with baking parchment.
- Flatten the rolls. Spray or drizzle them with water and then sprinkle on sesame seeds.
- Let rolls rise on the pan for 1 hour.
- Heat oven to 435°F. Bake buns for 20 minutes.

MAKES 6 BUNS

17.64 OUNCES (500 G) WATER

0.42 OUNCES (12 G) YEAST

2.46 OUNCES (70 G) CORNMEAL

4.58 OUNCES (130 G) RICE FLOUR

5.29 OUNCES (150 G) BUCKWHEAT FLOUR

1 TEASPOON SALT

0.52 OUNCES (15 G) FIBER HUSKS

CANOLA OIL FOR YOUR HANDS

SESAME SEEDS TO SPRINKLE OVER THE BUNS

Hamburgers

Authentic hamburgers are really juicy and good. The smoked chili dressing brings out the grilled flavor of the meat. The garnishes for the burgers are important, but, most important of all, is using the best quality meat. We think that prime rib is especially good for burgers and prefer it coarsely ground. The meat should be consumed the same day as it was ground so it is best to grind the meat yourself.

- Coarsely grind the beef. If you don't have a meat grinder, ask for help at the meat market.
- Shape the ground beef into 4 equal-size burgers; salt and pepper the patties on each side. Leave patties at room temperature while you make the dressing.
- Finely chop the onion and put into a bowl. Blend in the mayonnaise, crème fraiche, ketchup, smoked paprika powder, salt, sambal oelek and cayenne pepper.
- Fry the bacon until crispy and lay on paper towels to absorb excess oil.
- Fry or grill the burgers on high heat to desired doneness. We recommend that you cook the burgers so that the meat stays pink on the inside for extra moisture.
- While the burgers are still very hot, top with cheese and bacon so the cheese will melt.
- Spread the dressing on the buns and add the burgers. Garnish with lettuce, sliced tomatoes, onion slices, pickle and more dressing before you add the top of the bun.

MAKES 4 HAMBURGERS
2.2 LBS PRIME RIB
SALT AND PEPPER
8 SLICES OF BACON
8 SLICES OF MATURE CHEESE
4 HAMBURGER BUNS (SEE
  PAGE 117)

SMOKED CHILI DRESSING
1 CLOVE GARLIC
2 TABLESPOONS MAYONNAISE
  (SEE PAGE 121)
5.07 OUNCES (1 1/2 DL)
  CRÈME FRAICHE
1 TABLESPOON KETCHUP
1 TEASPOON SMOKED PAPRIKA
  POWDER
½ TEASPOON SALT
½ TEASPOON SAMBAL OELEK
¼ TEASPOON CAYENNE PEPPER

GARNISHING
1 HEAD ICEBERG LETTUCE
2 TOMATOES
1 RED ONION
2 SMALL PICKLES

Béarnaise Sauce

Nothing beats a homemade béarnaise sauce and it's not as hard to make as many believe! Gather your courage and try. All you need are patience and good quality ingredients. When making béarnaise sauce for the first time, make sure you have no distractions because it's easy to lose focus and then the sauce will separate.

- Finely chop the shallot.
- Mix the shallot, tarragon, white wine vinegar, and water in a saucepan.
- Put the pan on the stovetop and heat mixture until it comes to simmer and reduces for 2 minutes.
- Remove pan from heat.
- Put the butter into a fresh saucepan.
- Melt the butter over medium high heat, stirring constantly with a wisp until the butter browns.
- The butter is ready when it is golden brown and smells nutty.
- Remove butter from the heat.
- Whisk the egg yolks into the saucepan with the tarragon reduction.
- Put the saucepan on a burner at medium heat and stir constantly until the egg yolks are airy, slightly warmed and steamy.
- Add the butter in a thin stream as you stir vigorously over low heat. It is important that the mixture not heat too much, so be prepared to remove the saucepan from the heat if the sauce shows signs of separating and doesn't look completely smooth any longer.
- When all the butter has been blended in, the sauce is ready. If the sauce is still too thin, continue stirring at medium heat until the mixture thickens. Be careful because it can become too warm and separate. Salt and pepper sauce to taste.
- Serve immediately.

MAKES 1 PORTION

1 SHALLOT

1 TABLESPOON DRIED TARRAGON

1 TABLESPOON WHITE WINE VINEGAR

1.69 OUNCES (1/2 DL) WATER

6.34 OUNCES (180 G) BUTTER

2 EGG YOLKS

SALT AND PEPPER

TIP!
If the sauce separates, begin again with a new egg yolk in a clean saucepan; whisk yolk until foamy. Now whisk in the separated sauce in a thin stream instead of the butter. Another solution is to throw in an ice cube to cool the sauce if you notice that it is on the verge of separating.

Mayonnaise

Too many people think that it is hard to make good mayonnaise so they decide to buy ready-made instead. Homemade mayonnaise just takes a few ingredients and most of us already have those ingredients at home. It isn't just easy to make your own mayonnaise, it's also amazingly good!

- Whisk the egg yolk, Dijon mustard, red wine vinegar, and salt together in a large bowl.
- Whisk in the oil as you pour it in a thin stream. Whisk constantly so the egg yolk and oil will combine properly for a creamy mayonnaise.

<u>MAKES 1 PORTION</u>
1 EGG YOLK
1 TABLESPOON DIJON MUSTARD
1 TEASPOON RED WINE VINEGAR
¼ TEASPOON SALT
6.76 OUNCES (2 DL) CANOLA OIL

<u>TIP!</u>
Use this mayonnaise for the filling in the sandwich tart, in the dressing for the hamburgers or for our super good picnic rolls!

Pizza

Pizza dough with crispy edges that's easy to roll out thin in the cornmeal. Perfect for Friday night pizza.

- Whisk the yeast into the water.
- Add the remaining ingredients and mix until dough is smooth.
- Cover the bowl with plastic wrap and let dough rise for 2 hours.
- Divide the dough into 4 equal-sized pieces and roll each out on a work surface covered well with cornmeal.
- Spread tomato sauce over each pizza and top with grated cheese and your favorite toppings.
- Heat oven to 475°F. Bake pizzas on a baking sheet covered with parchment for 5-10 minutes.

PIZZA DOUGH FOR 4 PIZZAS

0.35 OUNCES (10 G) YEAST
14.10 OUNCES (400 G) COLD WATER
1.76 OUNCES (50 G) RICE FLOUR
0.70 OUNCES (20 G) CORNMEAL
3.17 OUNCES (90 G) BUCKWHEAT F
2.11 OUNCES (60 G) CORNSTARCH
½ TEASPOON SALT
0.52 OUNCES (15 G) FIBER HUSKS
  (GROUND PSYLLIUM SEED HUSKS)
CORNMEAL FOR ROLLING OUT
TOMATO SAUCE
GRATED CHEESE
YOUR FAVORITE TOPPINGS

Tomato Sauce

Homemade pizza deserves a good tomato sauce. This is our version.

- Press the garlic.
- Quickly sauté the garlic and tomato purée with the olive oil in a saucepan.
- Pour in the chopped tomatoes, salt, pepper, herbs, and sugar.
- Simmer the sauce for at least 20 minutes.

MAKES 1 PORTION SAUCE

2 CLOVES GARLIC
2 TABLESPOONS TOMATO
  PURÉE
3 TABLESPOONS OLIVE OIL
1 CAN CHOPPED TOMATOES
SALT
BLACK PEPPER
2 TEASPOONS DRIED HERBS
½ TABLESPOON SUGAR

Divide the dough into 4 equal-sized pieces.

Shape each piece into a ball.

Roll out each piece into a circle on a work surface well-covered with cornmeal.

Spread tomato sauce over each of the pizzas and top with grated cheese. Add your favorite toppings.

Dill Muffins

*Dill muffins are a good combination with
crayfish as an appetizer. You can also serve
them with fish soup. Bake these little breads
in a muffin pan. Make sure the bread has cooled
completely before you add the cheese sauce.*

- Heat oven to 400°F.
- Finely chop the dill.
- Whisk all the ingredients together and blend
  to a smooth batter.
- Let the batter rest for about 15 minutes.
- Line muffin pan with muffin cups or oil well.
  Pour the batter into 5 muffin cups.
- Bake for about 20 minutes.
- Let cool.
- Grate the cheese and blend it with the crème
  fraiche. Refrigerate until serving time.
- Top muffins with Västerbotten cheese sauce.
  Decorate with 1-2 crayfish tails and a bit of
  fresh dill.

MAKES 5 MUFFINS
0.52 OUNCES (15 G) DILL,
    ABOUT 1 JAR FULL
7.05 OUNCES (200 G) COLD
    MILK
1 EGG
0.70 OUNCES (20 G) BUTTER
½ TEASPOON BAKING POWDER
2.46 OUNCES (70 G) BUCKWHEAT
    FLOUR
½ TEASPOON SALT
0.35 OUNCES (10 G) PSYLLIUM
    SEED HUSKS

VÄSTERBOTTEN CHEESE SAUCE
5.29 OUNCES (150 G) VÄSTER-
    BOTTEN CHEESE (A SWEDISH
    HARD COW'S MILK CHEESE,
    AGED 12-14 MONTHS AND
    SOMEWHAT SIMILAR TO PARME-
    SAN CHEESE)
6.76 OUNCES (2 DL) CRÈME
    FRAICHE

TOPPING
5 - 10 CRAYFISH TAILS
FRESH DILL

Lingonberry Loaf

Although this is a pretty loaf, the sourness from the buttermilk and lingonberries cuts the sweetness of the syrup. Add the berries while still frozen to prevent the whole loaf from turning pink.

- Whisk together the buttermilk, yeast, and syrup.
- Add the buckwheat flour, salt, bread spices, psyllium seed husks, and buckwheat flakes.
- Fold in the lingonberries carefully so they don't split.
- Sprinkle work surface with buckwheat flour. Form dough into a rectangular loaf to fit a 1½-quart bread pan.
- Let dough rise in the prepared pan for about 3 hours.
- Heat oven to 400°F.
- Bake bread for 60 minutes.
- Cool bread completely before cutting.

MAKES 1 LOAF

35.27 OUNCES (1000 G) BUTTERMILK

1.05 OUNCES (30 G) YEAST

7.05 OUNCES (200 G) SYRUP

15.52 OUNCES (440 G) BUCKWHEAT FLOUR

2 TEASPOONS SALT

3 TEASPOONS BREAD SPICES

1.05 OUNCES (30 G) PSYLLIUM SEED HUSKS

1.41 OUNCES (40 G) BUCKWHEAT FLAKES

3.52 OUNCES (100 G) FROZEN LINGONBERRIES (CRANBERRIES CAN BE SUBSTITUTED)

BUCKWHEAT FLOUR FOR SPRINKLING OVER THE LOAF

Butter Bean Dip

Here's a super tasty dip that goes perfectly with crunchy crisp bread or on toast topped with a couple slices of roast beef.

- If the beans are canned, rinse well in cold water.
- Brown the butter in a saucepan until it is golden and has a nutty smell. Stir the butter constantly to prevent burning.
- Chop the shallot.
- Blend the beans, butter, shallot, tarragon, and salt. Process in a blender until smooth and creamy.
- The dip is now ready to serve. Store in the refrigerator. When the dip is cold, it will have a firmer consistency.

MAKES 1 PORTION
8.46 OUNCES (240 G)
  COOKED BUTTER BEANS
  (LARGE WHITE BEANS)
3.52 OUNCES (100 G)
  BUTTER
1 SHALLOT
1 TABLESPOON TARRAGON
½ TEASPOON SALT

Chanterelle Mushroom Sandwich

There are many ways to make good chanterelle mushroom sandwiches - every mushroom hunter has her own favorite recipe. This one is a real winner. You can prepare this for a light lunch or an appetizer at a fall party.

- Chop the onion and garlic.
- Fry the mushrooms, onion, and garlic in the butter.
- Mix the mushrooms (saving a few for topping the sandwiches), onion, garlic, crème fraiche, thyme, black pepper, and salt.
- Bring a large pan of water to rolling boil.
- While water comes to boil, crack each egg into a small bowl and sprinkle each with a tablespoon of vinegar. Let eggs rest for 5 minutes.
- Swirl the water to create a little whirl-pool; pour 1 egg into the vortex at the center of whirlpool and lower heat to a gentle boil. Cook the egg in the water for about 3 minutes. The white should be completely firm when you carefully poke the egg. The yellow should be loose. Now the egg is perfect. Spoon out egg carefully and place the egg on a plate while you poach the other egg the same way.
- Toast the bread.
- Grate the cheese.
- Spread a layer of mushroom cream on each slice of bread, sprinkle on the grated cheese, add poached egg, and top with thyme and the butter-fried chanterelles.
- Serve immediately.

MAKES 2 SANDWICHES

½ YELLOW ONION

1 CLOVE GARLIC

3.52 OUNCES (100 G) CHANTERELLE MUSHROOMS

2 TABLESPOONS BUTTER

½ TABLESPOON CRÈME FRAICHE

2 THYME SPRIGS

BLACK PEPPER

SALT

2 EGGS

2 TABLESPOONS VINEGAR ESSENCE (12%)

2 SLICES FRENCH LOAF (SEE PAGE 93)

3.38 OUNCES (1 DL) GRATED VÄSTERBOTTEN CHEESE (A SWEDISH HARD COW'S MILK CHEESE, AGED 12-14 MONTHS AND SOMEWHAT SIMILAR TO PARMESAN CHEESE)

Apple Marmalade
with Cardamom

One of the best ways to savor fall apples is to make marmalade with them – it really brings out their flavor and beauty. We like to keep the peel on the apples for extra flavor, color, and consistency. Cardamom enhances the flavor and the whole seeds brighten up the marmalade.

- Cut the apples into small cubes and discard the seeds and pit.
- Pour the apples, sugar, cardamom, and water into a heavy saucepan.
- Simmer the mixture over medium heat for about 10 minutes or until the apples are soft and slightly transparent.
- Pour the marmalade into clean glass jars. Store in refrigerator.

MAKES 1 PORTION

17.63 OUNCES (500 G) SWEDISH APPLES WITH PITS REMOVED; A SOUR TYPE OF APPLE RECOMMENDED

12.34 OUNCES (350 G) SUGAR

1 TEASPOON WHOLE CARDAMOM SEEDS

3.38 OUNCES (1 DL) WATER

TIP!
It is important that the jars are very clean. Wash and rinse them well or fill them with boiling water to kill all the bacteria. Fill the jars to the brim with marmalade, keeping in mind that the marmalade will be extremely hot as you pour. Place the lid on the jars immediately after filling to create a vacuum that will help preserve the marmalade longer.

Teacakes

Soft, tasty teacakes are a favorite with many people. They go well with a cup of tea, particularly when you are curled up in the corner of the sofa with a book.

- Whisk the yeast into the milk.
- Add the remaining ingredients and stir until dough is evenly mixed.
- Cover the bowl with plastic wrap and let dough rise for about 3 hours.
- Oil your hands and work surface well.
- Cut the dough into 8 pieces and roll into balls.
- Cover baking sheet with baking parchment. Lay rolls on the baking pan and flatten them. Prick tops if desired.
- Heat oven to 400°F.
- Let teacakes rise on the baking sheet for about 30 minutes.
- Bake for 15 minutes.
- Cool completely before cutting.

MAKES 8 TEACAKES

0.42 OUNCES (12 G) YEAST

17.63 OUNCES (500 G) MILK

0.70 OUNCES (20 G) OIL

0.70 OUNCES (20 G) SYRUP

3.52 OUNCES (100 G) OAT FLOUR

4.93 OUNCES (140 G) BUCKWHEAT FLOUR

1 TEASPOON SALT

½ TEASPOON BREAD SPICES

0.70 OUNCES (20 G) FIBER HUSKS

OIL FOR YOUR HANDS WHEN PREPARING BREAD.

The Dietician's Page

My name is Karolina Byström. I am a dietician and have calculated the nutritional values for the breads in this book. In my work, I meet people who have gluten intolerance and need advice about what to eat. Most feel that bread is the hardest food to give up. They don't think that the gluten-free alternatives at the grocery stores are any good. Those who have tried to bake gluten-free at home say that the dough is difficult to handle, dry, and boring. To be able to recommend a book with gluten-free breads that are just as good as "regular" bread is ever so cool. That the breads are baked with masses of nutrition-rich ingredients full of minerals, proteins, and good fats is a huge plus factor.

About 1% of the Swedish population is gluten-intolerant (the condition is called celiac disease). Celiac is an auto-immune disease, which means that the body builds antibodies, in this case, against the gluten protein in wheat called gliadin. Rye and barley have proteins like gliadin and, unfortunately, the antibodies fight against them also. If you are gluten-intolerant and ingest gluten, the body produces antibodies that cause an inflammation in the small intestine. The inside of the small intestine is covered with tiny, tiny villi whose purpose is to absorb nutritious elements from the food we eat. The ville tissues are injured by the inflammation, which means that their ability to take up important elements such as iron, calcium, vitamin B-12 and folic acid is decreased. In turn, this can lead to depriving those with gluten-intolerance of these important vitamins. The most common symptoms connected to a vitamin deficiency are osteoporosis, tiredness, diarrhea, and constipation. In children, these deficiencies can lead to delayed development and gluten-intolerance is often discovered in connection with that. In adults, the symptoms are often more diffuse, which makes the condition more difficult to diagnose. For that reason, it is common for people to go a long time without a diagnosis. It can be a period of ten years from the first symptoms to diagnosis.

Through research, we know that this disease is inherited. The risk of inheriting it from your parents is about 10%. We also know that gluten-intolerance is twice as common among women as men, as for all auto-immune diseases. The rate of celiac disease has risen sharply in recent decades, so the latest studies have also considered environmental factors.

Gluten-intolerance is not curable and one doesn't grow out of it, but, if you avoid anything containing gluten, the symptoms disappear. After just a few weeks of gluten-free eating, you will feel better and, after a few months, the damage to the small intestine should be repaired.

If you suspect that you are gluten-intolerant, you should see your doctor. Blood tests will indicate whether or not your body is producing antibodies against gluten. If the result is positive, have your intestines tested. If you suspect that you are gluten-intolerant, it is important that you do not begin a gluten-free diet on your own initiative because the blood tests won't be able to reveal whether or not you have celiac disease.

If you have been diagnosed with celiac disease, it is very important to keep your diet gluten-free. Most gluten-intolerant people have to make big changes in their diet because gluten is in so many common food basics. I think it is important that gluten-free food be as much like "regular" food as possible, which isn't always easy to accomplish. For that reason, it is always pleasing when you find a good gluten-free alternative, such as the recipes in this book.

Dietician
Karolina Byström

Nutritional values per 3.5 oz. / 100 gram

	(Kcal) Calories	Carbohydrates	Protein	Fat	Saturated fat	Monounsaturated fat	Polyunsaturated fat	Fiber	Iron	Folic acid	Calcium	Sodium	Sugar
guette	147	31 g	3.0 g	0.7 g	0.1 g	0.2 g	0.2 g	3.2 g	0.7 mg	32.3 ug	5.1 mg	376 mg	0.16 g
kwheat rolls	129	20.8 g	3.5 g	3.3 g	0.6 g	1.1 g	1.4 g	11.6 g	2.5 mg	28.8 ug	6.0 mg	278 mg	0.1 g
issant	391	28 g	9.5 g	26.5 g	15 g	7.1 g	3.0 g	6.6 g	0.8 mg	24 ug	165 mg	425 mg	4.6 g
aish	185	24 g	4.9 g	7.0 g	0.7 g	1.4 g	4.5 g	8.0 g	1.2 mg	30 ug	27 mg	268 mg	3.3 g
ll muffins	192	20 g	6.0 g	9.3 g	5.0 g	2.6 g	0.6 g	3.3 g	1.1 mg	25 ug	190 mg	607 mg	0g
ench loaf	179	20 g	7.0 g	7.0g	2.0 g	2.9 g	1.9 g	8.4 g	1.2 mg	39 ug	100 mg	241 mg	0.42 g
ed Rolls	149	31 g	2.9 g	0.6 g	0.2 g	0.2 g	0.2 g	2.4 g	0.6 mg	22 ug	4.6 mg	227 mg	0.2 g
arse rolls	122	23.7 g	3.4 g	1.1 g	0.2 g	0.1 g	0.4 g	4.4 g	0.4 mg	22.5 ug	1.9 mg	0.7 mg	0.3 g
arse bread	222	4.7 g	8.9 g	18.6 g	1.6 g	2.7 g	6.5 g	8.5 g	2.3 mg	44 ug	18 mg	262 mg	0.2 g
mburger buns	199	25 g	6.7 g	7.5g	1.9 g	2.7 g	1.7 g	7.8 g	0.5 mg	33 ug	90 mg	60 mg	2.75 g
ncakes	220	24 g	7.8 g	9.8 g	11 g	2.8 g	5.2 g	5.2 g	2.0 mg	25 ug	35.5 mg	302 mg	3.6 g
Crisp bread	160	34 g	3.2 g	0.7 g	0.1 g	0.2 g	0.2 g	0.5 g	0.6 mg	21 ug	5.1 mg	310 mg	0.1 g
ristmas bread	211	33.7 g	5.8 g	5.7 g	3.1 g	1.2 g	0.3 g	3.9 g	0.7 mg	22 ug	143 mg	309 mg	0.1 g
ecial Christmas bread	170	31 g	4.7 g	2.2 g	0.3 g	0.8 g	0.8 g	5.9 g	1.8 mg	39 ug	18 mg	351 mg	2.7 g
lar French rolls	211	32 g	4.6 g	0.6 g	0.1 g	0.2 g	0.2 g	3.i g	0.9 mg	32 ug	5.3 mg	426 mg	0.1 g
urdough bread	218	44 g	7.3g	2.1 g	1.0 g	0.4 g	0.3 g	5.1 g	1.0 mg	19.7 ug	61 mg	72 mg	4.8 g
axseed rolls	150	32 g	4.6 g	0.6 g	0.1 g	0.2 g	0.2 g	3.1 g	0.9 mg	32 ug	5.3 mg	426 mg	0.1 g
rn muffins	187	39.7 g	3.6 g	0.8 g	0.1 g	0.2 g	0.3 g	1.6 g	1.4 mg	15 ug	24.2 mg	174 mg	0.3 g
rrot bread	134	26 g	3.1 g	1.6 g	0.2 g	0.3 g	0.6 g	2.9 g	0.8 mg	25.8 ug	6.2 mg	1.1 mg	0.1 g
zza dough	249	48 g	5.9 g	3.2 g	1.8 g	0.8 g	0.3 g	3.1 g	0.9 mg	42 ug	101 mg	562 mg	5.9 g
tato/goji berry	162	15 g	3.1 g	9.6 g	1.6 g	6.3 g	0.9 g	3.7 g	0.5 mg	12.6 ug	120 mg	391 mg	0.2 g
isin buns	150	31.5 g	2.9 g	0.7 g	0.2 g	0.2 g	0.1 g	2.8 g	0.7 mg	29 ug	7.0 mg	349 mg	0.5 g
ones	190	41.5 g	4.0 g	0.7 g	0.1 g	0.2 g	0.2 g	3.4 g	0.8 mg	24.3 ug	5.6 mg	223 mg	0.1 g
rup Limpa	200	38 g	4.9 g	2.4 g	2.4 g	0.5 g	0.2 g	3.1 g	0.8 mg	35 ug	69 mg	501 mg	1.9 g
tter rolls	193	38 g	5.0 g	2.6 g	1.4 g	0.6 g	0.3 g	4.5 g	1.0 mg	36.1 ug	82.4 mg	578 mg	1.3 g
nflower seed rolls	261	20 g	9.6 g	15 g	7.7 g	3.5 g	2.6 g	4.1 g	0.8 mg	7.6 ug	273 mg	136 mg	1.4 g
out bread	211	42 g	4.4 g	2.3 g	1.2 g	0.6 g	0.2 g	4.4 g	1.3 mg	31 ug	71 mg	744 mg	4.0 g
ltan	191	36 g	4.7 g	4.7 g	1.3 g	0.6 g	0.2 g	3.2 g	0.7 mg	23.5 ug	75 mg	172 mg	1.6 g
ncakes	186	27 g	6.7 g	5.2 g	0.6 g	1.2 g	3.0 g	5.5 g	1.3 mg	44.8 ug	30 mg	242 mg	0.5 g
rtillas	220	41.2 g	5.4 g	3.4 g	1.4 g	0.8 g	0.8 g	3.0 g	0.8 mg	12.6 ug	83.8 mg	668 mg	9.2 g
in bread	252	36 g	5.8 g	8.6 g	1.6 g	3.8 g	2.6 g	4.0 g	1.8 mg	35.4 ug	86 mg	194 mg	4.4 g
	234	30.6 g	6.8 g	9.0 g	1.4 g	2.6 g	4.6 g	4.6 g	2.6 mg	38 ug	19.2 mg	282 mg	3.0 g
	200	29 g	5.7 g	6.3 g	1.8 g	2.6 g	1.4 g	4.1 g	1.2 mg	32 ug	92 mg	489 mg	1.1 g
	139	29 g	2.7 g	0.5 g	o g	0.2 g	0.2 g	6.2 g	0.3 mg	3.0 ug	106 mg	323 mg	0.3 g
	242	21 g	14 g	9.6 g	2.7 g	2.6 g	3.7 g	8.9 g	2.2 mg	49.6 ug	166 mg	405 mg	0.9 g

ACKNOWLEDGMENTS

This book would not be the same if it weren't for the input of many wonderful people. We are eternally grateful!

First and foremost, we must thank each other because we respected each other's ideas and didn't set any boundaries. We dared to "just do it." We struggled with the development of the recipes even when half of them landed in the trash bin and we laughed through half of the book.

Thank you, respectively, to Martin and Jimmy because they supported us and our chatter about the book, day in and day out, and Maria's children, Mira and Felix, because you tirelessly tested every bread experiment.

Thank you to Electrolux and, most of all, Johanna Hallander and Gabriella Picano, who let us borrow the test kitchen several times. Without you we would never have managed to test so many recipes in such a short time.

Thanks to our first tasters, Mia Öhrn and Johan Jureskog – without you we might not have believed in our ideas and continued.

Thanks to Rick Carlberg and Hanna Blohm for their valuable feedback.

Thanks to Karin Ädelsköld who sent us to the fantastic Heidi-Maria Wallinder.

Thank you to Forma Books, Ica Publishers and the lovely Heidi-Maria, without you there would not have been a book at all, just a pile of paper in a box. We would also like to thank Carin Brosten because you came in and brought everything to fruition.

Thank you lovely Filippa Tredal for the beautiful pictures and an unforgettable photo week.

Thanks to Eva and Gustav Kvie for allowing us to live and photograph in your wonderful house on Gotland.

Thank you Ulla Blohm, Gunlög Israelsson, Bertil Jonsson and Monica Nilson for suggesting the requisites to us.

Thank you Mikael Engblom for the fantastic layout.

Thanks to Karolina Byström for calculating the nutritional values of every bread recipe and your fine, enlightening text about gluten-intolerance. You are a pearl!

And a big thank you to everyone in our circle who believed in us, encouraged us, and helped us in every way possible!

Index